CHEAPER

BALLANTINE BOOKS

NEW YORK

RICK DOBLE *and* TOM PHILBIN

CHEAPER

Insiders' Tips

FOR

SAVING

ON

Everything

Cheaper is a commonsense guide to personal finance. In practical advice books, as in life, there are no guarantees, and readers are cautioned to rely on their own judgment about their individual circumstances and to act accordingly.

A Ballantine Books Trade Paperback Original

Copyright © 2009 by Rick Doble and Tom Philbin

Published in the United States by Ballantine Books,
an imprint of The Random House Publishing Group,
a division of Random House, Inc., New York.

BALLANTINE and colophon are registered trademarks
of Random House, Inc.

LIBRARY OF CONGRESS CATALOGING-IN-PUBLICATION DATA
Doble, Rick.
Cheaper: insiders' tips for saving on everything /
Rick Doble and Tom Philbin.
p. cm.
Includes bibliographical references.
ISBN 978-0-345-51208-6 (pbk.)
1. Consumer education.   2. Shopping.   3. Finance, Personal.
I. Philbin, Tom, 1934– .   II. Title.
TX335.D619 2009
640.73—dc22   2008055709

Printed in the United States of America

www.ballantinebooks.com

2 4 6 8 9 7 5 3 1

Book design by Barbara M. Bachman

CONTENTS

PART 2
Insiders' Tips for Saving Money on Specific Products and Services

AUTHORS' NOTE

INTRODUCTION

*H*ERE'S THE SITUATION THAT JUST ABOUT EVERYONE HAS BEEN dealing with, including the authors of this book. You know that you work hard, but you seem to be spinning your wheels or getting stuck in the mud. You work long hours, yet your family's income has stayed flat while prices have been skyrocketing. This "financial squeeze" has put millions of Americans in a stranglehold.

So what do you do? You could take another job, but then Americans already work one hundred hours longer per year than just about any other workers in the industrialized world. In addition, during the last seven years your real income (adjusted for inflation) dropped $1,175 at a time when average families are spending $4,655 more for everything from gas to food to housing to health insurance.

But wait—the news gets worse. While the price of gas has been mostly bad news, add to that the price of heating oil and propane gas. The federal Energy Information Administration projected a 34 percent increase for 2009.

If you feel you are working harder, getting paid less, and still having to shell out more money, join the club. Just about everyone in the middle is feeling the pain.

So is there anything that you can do about this? The answer is a resounding yes—and in this book we'll show you how.

Sometimes money matters can be as exciting to read as a tract on solid-waste management. But the bottom line, as it were, is that the facts can mean the difference in whether someone walks to work or drives a car, has a warm coat for a winter's day, or is able to give their kids a Christmas toy. Sometimes money is the difference between life and death, as when somebody doesn't go to a doctor, or has to make a choice between medicine and food, or medicine and electricity.

The authors have always thought that the highest-quality information comes from people who have a kind of dirty-fingernail grasp of it: the insiders, the people who work in a particular field and know where the bodies are buried. For example, the writer in the funeral trade magazine who tells you why it's stupid to pay hundreds of dollars for a concrete liner box, the executive at Johns Hopkins Hospital who can tell you whom to negotiate with to glean a possible 30 percent savings on a hospital bill, the professional engineer who counsels that 98 percent of all wet-basement problems stem from excess water saturating a house foundation, the auto mechanic who tells you that using cruise control can save you 14 percent in gas costs, and the authors themselves: One of them, Tom Philbin, has written three books on saving money and has long had a passion for helping consumers, and the other, Rick Doble, founder of SavvyDiscounts.com, is equally motivated and one of the greatest hagglers there is. The authors know where some bodies are buried as well.

Most of this book contains tips from such insiders, but we have included some other fairly well-known money-saving ideas as well, such as ways to save when buying gardening supplies. The only criterion a tip must meet for inclusion in this book is that it will save readers money.

The book is divided into two parts. First are overall shopping tips, general approaches that will help you achieve discounts—such as shopping around, haggling (which 67 percent of shoppers, possibly more, now do), and buying store brands—and that will make you aware of strategies, such as upselling and suggestive selling, that sales personnel use to separate you from more of your money. The second part is an A-to-Z lineup of a wide variety of specific products and services, with suggestions on how to trim—and in many cases slash—the cost of staple items such as drugs, food, clothing, gasoline, and oil. But we also include offbeat items such as pianos and chimney cleaning. Both sections of the book are also informed by the authors' keen awareness that people and businesses will try to rip you off. Indeed, just in the home improvement category, homeowners will learn how they can save literally tens of thousands of dollars. At the end of each section is a summary of money-saving strategies that should help you get a better grasp of things.

We have mapped out nearly twenty categories where it's simple to save money: from electricity to fuel oil, from auto insurance to groceries. The savings can be substantial and can easily add up to $5,000. And $5,000 is just about the right amount of money to help pay for the extra cost of gasoline and other added expenses you have no control over. Plus, if you follow all of our tips, we believe you can save a lot more than $5,000, but just to be conservative (we'd rather offer you less and deliver more), we'll say $5,000.

We are proud of this compendium of useful and easy tips. It took coauthors Tom Philbin and Rick Doble a combined thirty years to discover, research, and test out a variety of money-saving ideas before settling on these very best— simple and easy—ways to save money that won't take you any more time and won't change your lifestyle.

Every one of our tips is backed up by thorough research. We quote and refer to the most reliable authorities we have found in each field to demonstrate the truth and practicality of our tips and the amounts of money that you can save.

One point should be stressed: It is important to get into

the habit of using money-saving tips. Ideally, you will get into that habit, and as you do, you will notice that you go to the gas pump less frequently, or have saved 30 percent on your food bill, or hundreds on a doctor's bill. We believe it's a habit you'll be glad you got into.

All our best,
Rick Doble and
Tom Philbin

PART

1.

Overall
Shopping Tips

THERE ARE A VARIETY OF STRATEGIES AND MARKETING TRICKS THAT YOU SHOULD BE AWARE OF TO ENHANCE YOUR ABILITIES AS A SHOPPER. KNOWING THESE WILL, OF COURSE, HELP YOU GET PRODUCTS AND SERVICES AT A HEALTHY DISCOUNT. THE FOLLOWING IS A ROUNDUP OF SIXTEEN OF THESE FROM THE AUTHORS' OWN EXPERIENCES AND FROM INDUSTRY INSIDERS.

...

SHOPPING TIP #1: SHOP AROUND

IN SHOPPING AROUND, YOUR GOAL, OF COURSE, IS TO FIND OUT who is selling the product or service you want the cheapest, and to gather those prices. Your three tools are the telephone, the Internet, and the yellow pages. All are invaluable sources for determining the cost of the product or service from various companies.

We find the telephone works quite well. And please don't believe the myth that retailers won't give you prices over the phone. The vast majority will. And why not? The bottom line is the bottom line: They want to make money, and they'll facilitate that any way they can.

Just call, ask if they have the item (or service), and then ask the price. It is important to know exactly what you want so you can transmit it to the seller in language he or she under-stands. In some cases—such as with bath fixtures, light fix-tures, and power tools—knowing the model number will be essential, and that is something you can get from the manu-facturer's website, flyers, or catalog. In almost all cases we predict that you will get the price easily, particularly in these recessionary times. Yet if you are chary about being so direct, then you can be a little more artful in your query. Following is one good technique.

First, ask if the retailer if he or she has such-and-such a product. Even if you know that they do, play dumb.

When they say yes, then you say:

"How much would that cost?"

You'll usually get the answer instantly, although some-times the retailer will go off the phone to check the shelves or the rack to get the price. Sometimes, when they won't give the price (a rare occurrence), I use another technique: "I would re-ally appreciate knowing the cost. I don't want to travel over there if I can't afford it."

Don't ask us why they usually give the price information when you ask about the product availability. Maybe it's be-cause the focus of the first question is not on price but prod-uct, and maybe it's because you don't make it sound like you know precisely about such things. Either way, it's a technique we've used successfully for many years.

PRICE COMPARISONS VIA THE INTERNET

The Internet is a gold mine when it comes to comparison shopping. A number of sites, such as www.bizrate.com and www.pricegrabber.com, allow you to make comparisons for just about any product. Prices should be used only as bench-marks, because a company's return policy and shipping charges can add considerably to what may appear to be a very low price. However, these Web comparisons give you a good place to start. In addition, you can often go the manufacturer's site and find a complete description, spec sheet, a list of what is included with a purchase, etc. In addition you can find reviews and user comments at other websites. Often typing in the make and model of a product into Google will yield a wealth of information. If you decide to buy locally, print out prices and specifications you find on the Internet and take these with you to the local store. These can be a great help when trying to haggle a deal. With used items, past sales on eBay can give you a good idea of a fair price.

SHOPPING TIP #2: HAGGLE

ONCE YOU KNOW THE SELLER'S PRICE YOU CAN EITHER PURCHASE the item or service at that price, or haggle, that is, negotiate a lower price, something more people than ever before are doing these days. Two years ago, 33 percent of Americans haggled. Today, according to Britt Beemer of America's Research Group, that figure has gone up to 67 percent. And in a survey in late 2007, Consumers Union discovered that 61 percent of its readers haggled—and 90 percent of them were successful in getting discounts on furniture, electronic items, appliances, even medical bills. And yearly savings can run into thousands of dollars. Coauthor Rick Doble estimates that he saves $9,000 a year. (While your savings may not be as much, don't be discouraged. Remember, he's one of the country's most experienced hagglers.)

You can haggle virtually anywhere, including big department stores like Macy's, supermarket giants like Safeway, discount stores such as Kmart, and home improvement stores like Home Depot. The experience of Jay Lyons at Home Depot pretty much expresses the attitude of all big retailers. One day Lyons was in a Home Depot in Commack, New York, and saw a Kohler whirlpool that he liked, but it was selling for $1,200, a little too rich for him. "Plus, I figured," he told us, "this is Home Depot. They won't give a discount. They already have low prices." So he gave up, and started to price the whirlpool at other outlets. Home Depot was still the cheapest, so one day he returned and just on a lark asked the sales associate in the plumbing aisle, "What kind of a discount can you give me on that Kohler whirlpool?" He got a surprising response. "I don't know," the sales associate said. "How about $100?" "I was thinking more like $500," Lyons said. "No we can't do that," the associate said.

Lyons was silent, a great haggling strategy, though he didn't know it at the time, and the salesman finally broke the silence: "I think I can give you $350 off. Let me ask." He checked with his boss and that was the first of a number of days when Lyons asked big chains for good discounts—and got 'em.

PRODUCTS AND SERVICES YOU CAN ALWAYS HAGGLE FOR

Some products and services are easier to haggle for than others. Among the easiest are big-ticket items such as appliances, furniture, home improvement products (such as quality windows, doors, bath fixtures, kitchen cabinets), mattresses, cameras, TVs, gee-whiz digital equipment. The reason? They have a healthy profit margin and lowering the price a couple of hundred dollars isn't going to put the store in Chapter 11 bankruptcy. Most stores will not be willing to negotiate on the price of low-cost items because the profit margin is usually slim, but rules are made to be broken. Many a haggler has haggled small-ticket items.

It's a good idea to get a sense of what the markup is on products. Then when you negotiate, you are doing so from a knowledgeable position, and the seller will know this and know he has to "talk turkey" with you.

In general, big-ticket items carry a markup of 30 to 60 percent, but sometimes a lot more. For example, good quality kitchen cabinets are marked up a whopping 100 to 200 percent. And Janet Harriman, a jewelry dealer from Smyrna, North Carolina, says that commercial jewelry can carry a markup of 500 percent (500 is not a misprint!). Hence when you haggle such items, you will be haggling for hundreds and perhaps thousands of dollars in discounts.

The discounts can be, as suggested above, significant. For

example, with home improvement it has been our experience that you can get 30 percent off windows (including Andersen, Marvin, and other good brands), 25 percent off bath fixtures, 30 to 40 percent off kitchen and bath cabinets, 30 percent off skylights, and 50 percent off some light fixtures.

Hotel rooms are another easy area to haggle in. Hoteliers do it all the time. Figure an average reduction in room price of 10 to 25 percent but you could go higher as much as 40 percent, even in season. In the off season you can ask for even more. Remember, the hotelier is not making money when rooms are empty.

Bulk purchases are another easy area. For example, if you buy a case of wine or canned goods, or two or three pairs of pants instead of one, it should be no problem for retailers to trim the price 10 percent, and double that if you buy more than seven gallons of paint and ask for a "painter's discount" of 15 percent, or 10 percent on wall covering.

Another easy haggle is on used products, such as clothing. You may be able to get a discount of 5 percent to a whopping 85 percent, but you can also negotiate down things that are essentially already marked down, such as items marked "discontinued," on "clearance," or "closeout." How much? There is no set figure, but 50 percent is not unreasonable.

PRODUCTS AND SERVICES THAT OFTEN CAN BE HAGGLED OVER

There are some less obvious products and services that are also easy to haggle over. The most surprising of these is health care, such as getting discounts from doctors, dentists, pharmacists, even hospitals. A Harris Interactive poll in 2002 found that about 50 percent of all patients who asked for discounts got them.

What kind of a discount can you ask for? We would recommend that in the case of doctors, dentists, and pharmacists you ask for whatever your insurance company doesn't cover. Gerard Anderson, the director of the Johns Hopkins Center for Hospital Finance and Management, says, "The typical insurer gets about a 60 percent discount. If you go into the hospital and ask the chief financial officer, you may get a 30 percent discount, but you have to ask for it. It's totally up to the discretion of the CFO how much they or the person in the billing office are willing to give you."

You can also get food, including the essentials of most meals (meat and produce), near its "pull" or expiration date at around 50 percent off, and the more you purchase, the greater the discount. Any item, such as clothing, an appliance, or an electronics item, that is cosmetically marred is also often fair game for haggling. How much? We know that Wal-Mart and Kmart give 10 percent, but you may do better at other outlets. What are they going to do with it if they don't sell it?

Get to Know Your Store Managers

Have a nice friendly talk with the produce and meat managers and ask when the pull dates are and how much of the price will be cut.

For a discount on new clothing and shoes, Andy Dappen's book *Cheap Tricks* reveals the following markups: brand name, 50–55 percent; store brand, 60–80 percent; high fashion, 60–70 percent; brand-name shoes, 50 percent; private-label shoes, 60–70 percent. Here you can ask for a discount as high as your gut allows, or equal to the sale price on similar items sold in the past.

HAGGLING EXTRAS

While you naturally will be thinking cash savings when haggling, you can also negotiate "extras" or "freebies" that are not cash in hand but worth cash. For example Commack, New York, native Pete Prianti could not make a Sleepy's salesman budge on the $2,000 price of a mattress, but when Pete threatened to buy from Sleepy's archenemy, Bob's, the unbudgeable salesman budged. "He 'threw in' a free $600 headboard," says Pete, "and also gave us free delivery of the new mattress and no charge for hauling away the old one." There are many other freebies out there, usually based on some seller screwup, or a failure of service. Among some we know are a better-size hotel room when an original reserved room was not available, a larger rental car at the same price when a smaller reserved car was not available, or a better mattress when one ordered was not available.

Pushing the Right Button

When Sears delivered a dishwasher without the proper power adapter to the home of Jesse Birk in Hicksville, Long Island, Birk could have asked for a refund off the price. Yet Jesse, an experienced shopper, had learned from hard experience that such a request would have to route its way through the rapids of the company's accounting system, which would be difficult and likely mean a long delay. So instead Birk asked Sears to refund the price of the delivery ($50). This they did and he deposited the check within a week, and was able to purchase the adapter for $5.

HOW DO YOU ASK FOR A DISCOUNT?

As mentioned, you should have a sense of discounts and markups before going into the store. As you enter the store, scan the salespeople, and let your gut—a very accurate device—speak to you: Does one person in particular look like someone whom you could negotiate with successfully?

You should be friendly and gentle throughout when talking to the salespeople. Just tell them that you've looked over the item (say a dishwasher) and like it but think the price is a bit too steep. Can they give you a discount? If the answer is no, or the discount too low, ask to see the manager or other decision maker (call before you arrive to find this out) and ask him or her. If the answer is still no, ask if they can give you the item at its sales price. If the answer is still no, gently suggest that if you don't buy the item here you'll have to leave and buy it or a similar item at what you know to be their arch competitor. It's our bet that you will be successful.

Eight More Haggling Tips

- Never be enthusiastic about a price you get during haggling.
- Respond to offers with respectful silence—silence can be quite eloquent and persuasive.
- If you can, it's always easier to start haggling by noting some flaw in the product or service.
- When you can, pay cash to close a deal. It's a profoundly articulate persuader.
- Always approach the decision maker when they have time to talk.

- When considering buying a floor model, print out a list of the accessories from the Internet. If anything's missing, haggle away (coauthor Rick Doble got an already discounted Casio camera, marked down to $200, for $50 because some accessories, though unimportant, were missing).
- Keep your cool throughout.
- Use the Internet for an initial comparison and print out price and spec sheets.

Products and Services That Can Usually Be Haggled Over

- Big-ticket items
- Hotel rooms
- Bulk purchases
- Credit card interest rates
- Any product that is used
- Floor models marked for sale
- Heavily used new books
- Open packages
- Products marked "discontinued" or "clearance"

Products and Services That Can Often Be Haggled Over

- Health care
- Food about to reach its "pull" or expiration date
- An appliance or electronics item that is marred

- Imperfect clothing
- A service not performed as promised
  (can lead to "freebies")
- Freebies when a cash discount isn't available

#3

SHOPPING TIP #3:
TAKE ADVANTAGE OF
LOW-COST STORE BRANDS

ONE OF THE VERY BEST WAYS TO SAVE MONEY ON NEW PRODUCTS is to buy store brands instead of national brands. These brands (also called private labels) are available at just about every store and in every product category. Throughout this book, in fact, you will see us suggest that you buy store brands to save thousands of dollars every year. But in order to take advantage of these, keep in mind the following:

1. Store brands are brands made for that store and carried only in that store.
2. Just about every kind of store will have its own store brands, including hardware stores, drugstores, office supply stores, electronics stores, supermarkets, clothing stores—you name it.
3. The savings can be considerable—20 percent or more for everyday prices and up to 50 percent when on sale.

You may not be aware of the large selection of store brands in today's marketplace and the savings they can bring. For example, Wal-Mart has almost thirty of them. These brands cover food (Sam's Choice and Great Value), clothing such as Faded Glory and No Boundaries (NoBo), home furnishings such as HomeTrends and Mainstays, car batteries (EverStart), over-the-counter drugs (Equate), home electronics (Durabrand), outdoor equipment (Ozark Trail), vitamins (Spring Valley), and other products.

While store brands or "private labels" are a great way to

save money, there are other choices as well. Often there are lesser-known national brands as well as regional and even generic brands.

The term *off brand* is often used to distinguish other brands from the better-known national brands, but the term is a bit negative and off-putting. We prefer the term *alternative brand*. For example, Malt-O-Meal sells its cereals at a substantial discount just about everywhere in the country. It does very little advertising, and you will often find the bags of cereal on the bottom shelf. The company avoids paying for shelf placement as the expensive national brands do. As a result, the cost of the cereal is a good deal cheaper. We recommend store brands and private labels in particular because with the store's name behind them, the store is usually more than willing to refund your money.

The term *generic brand* applies to products that have no brand name. So a can of cola, for example, simply identifies itself as cola but with no accompanying brand name.

You may find *regional brands*, which are available only in your area of the country. These are often cheaper and just as good as national brands.

One tip: Whenever there is a unit price on the shelves, look at it. It measures costs using an apples-to-apples approach—for example, weight versus weight—and so you can quickly get an idea of what the best buy is.

#4

SHOPPING TIP #4:
BEST DEALS ARE IN A STORE'S SPECIALTY

THERE IS A LITTLE-KNOWN RULE OF THUMB THAT CAN SAVE YOU A ton of money: The very best deals are in the store's main product or service line, and the worst deals are generally in products or services that are not related to the store's principal sales. For example, at supermarkets, food products, their principal business, will be cheaper than at a drugstore, but personal care products will be cheaper at a drugstore than at a supermarket.

With stores selling more and more items outside their main line of business, one wonders where it will stop. (The next thing we expect is to see a surgeon wearing blood-flecked scrubs walking down an aisle. When someone stops him and asks him what he does, he'll answer: "I'm in aisle 6A. Open heart surgery.") But for now, to emphasize our point, you will generally get the best deal in office supplies at an office supply store, not in the stationery aisle at your supermarket; the best deal in cosmetics at a drugstore and not at a department store; the best deal on light-bulbs at a Wal-Mart type store and not a drugstore; the best deal on motor oil at an automotive store and not at a supermarket.

Rick compared the price of office supplies at a deep-discount department store with the price at an office supply store and found that he could save 51 percent by buying at the office supply store. These savings would also apply to school supplies during the back-to-school months.

When Rick compared the cost of nonfood items at a supermarket to the cost at a discount department store, he found that he saved 37 percent at the department store. When he compared pharmacy prices for nonpharmacy items to the prices at a discount department store, he found a huge difference—saving 84 percent at the department store versus the pharmacy.

#5 SHOPPING TIP #5:
DON'T BUY EXTENDED WARRANTIES

EXTENDED WARRANTIES HAVE GOT TO BE A MARKETER'S DREAM. Sell a service that may never be used—but the company gets to keep the money no matter what! Extended warranties also are something many consumers fall for (Rick even fell for it once): On the one hand you are buying a product with contradictory logic behind it. For example, you might be buying a TV, and are told it is reliable and a good deal—but on the other hand you are told that it might fail so you had better get an extended warranty to avoid any worry about repair costs if they happen to occur!

You don't need an extended warranty—say, one that covers repairs starting in the second year—because most products are covered by a standard warranty for the first year, and if a product is going to fail, it will most likely do so during that period. The extended warranty covers the years after the original warranty expires, the time period when the product is least likely to fail. As reported on the Fox Business website in September 2005, "Most extended warranties on appliances and electronic devices aren't worth it."

Also, if you buy an extended warranty, getting the company to honor its obligations may take a while. Rick bought an extended warranty for his father's television from Circuit City. When the TV did fail, unusually, during the extended warranty period, it took Circuit City three months to repair it. Repeated calls did not speed things up and Rick determined that since the company already had his money, it was in no hurry to fix the TV. Numerous other people have reported problems with repairs that were covered by extended warranties. In fact a brief search of the Internet brings up hundreds of complaints posted by consumers.

Despite the potent evidence against getting an extended warranty, many people will be unconvinced. Their logic: Why not just buy a warranty with each product so that you don't have to worry about being suddenly hit with a large repair expense? While there are always exceptions (a few people even beat the odds in Vegas), most people will do much better by simply shelling out the money when a repair is needed. This amount of cash should be much less than the combined cost of having a number of extended warranties. And remember, if you do insist on buying extended warranties, you had better have a great filing system so that you can verify your coverage years after you bought the item.

And there is another advantage to being extended-warrantyless: When you drop off your TV, let's say, for a repair, the repair department won't get your money until the repair is finished. So it's likely that you'll get that TV back a lot sooner than some sap who bought an extended warranty and now has no choice but to wait for the repair to be completed, since the company already has his money.

SHOPPING TIP #6:
COMPLAIN WHEN NECESSARY

ONE SUMMER SUNDAY IN 2008, A MAN NAMED JIM GORICK, WHO lives in Closter, New Jersey, unhappily discovered that some kids who had attended his son's birthday party had placed wet glasses on a small, valuable mahogany table and had stained it. Gorick had heard that you could remove such stains with a soft abrasive, such as pumice, and he was right. On the other hand, he didn't want to risk damaging the table permanently, so he took the table to a pro in a town about twenty-five miles away and agreed to get the top refinished for $75. The proprietor said he'd have the job done the following Friday, but when Gorick showed up, it wasn't ready. Gorick gently complained that this was an inconvenience to him, and the proprietor agreed to slash $25 off the fee and have it ready—for sure—the following Monday. And when Gorick showed up, the table had been beautifully refinished.

Here's another example: Saleswoman Jayne Matthews of Griffin, Georgia, had reserved a subcompact from Alamo car rental service for a weekend jaunt. But it wasn't available and when she complained she got the next-largest-size car—at no extra charge—and at a savings of $10 a day.

In another example, when a Holyoke, Massachusetts, couple (names withheld) went to the Bahamas, the air conditioner in their room sounded "like a cow in heat." They complained, and were upgraded to a much better room at no extra charge. It had a nicer view of the area—and no romantic cow.

What each of these customers did was complain about a service failure, and because of this they benefited. And that is Tip #6. If a product or service is not up to snuff, complain. Of course, you should not do it in a harsh or confrontational way, but just voice your concerns—to the manager or person in charge—and how you think you should get special treatment; in 99 out of 100 cases the manager will respond. Not that he's operating a charity. Rather, if he is smart, he will recognize that you are a customer, the lifeblood of his business, and the last thing he will want to do is make an adversary out of you.

COMPLAIN TO YOUR STATE ATTORNEY GENERAL'S OFFICE

One of the most effective ways to complain is to your state attorney general's office. While this office will not represent you or initiate legal action, it will add clout to your complaint.

Most attorney general's offices have a complaint form and a procedure to follow on their website. You must have full documentation and a reasonable request for your complaint to be handled by the attorney general's office.

This office will forward your complaint to the appropriate company and generally indicate that the office thinks your complaint has merit. This approval in itself often gets the attention of the company that the complaint was addressed to; in turn they will not want to be seen as unreasonable. And voilà! Very often your complaint will be resolved without further action. Look on the Internet for the website of the state office of your attorney general.

Small-Claims Court

*M*ost states now have a small-claims court that can handle disputes of up to $10,000. Check with your state for the exact dollar limit in your area. In such a court you represent yourself, so you do not have to pay any lawyer's fees. However, make sure that you bring complete documentation with you to court. Otherwise you will most likely lose your case.

SHOPPING TIP #7:
TAKE ADVANTAGE OF SEASONAL SALES

BUYING BIG THINGS WHEN THEY'RE ON SALE CAN SAVE YOU A tremendous amount of money. Typical sales discounts run from 20 to 40 percent or more, and "clearance" sales can have even greater discounts.

Happily, sale times are not all over the lot, but tend to be cyclical and seasonal, with many happening at about the same time every year. The exact timing may vary depending on the climate and area of the country where you live, but when you see an ad for an "annual sale" you can bet on that sale returning the following year. To find out when a sale is going to occur, ask salespeople for dates of their annual sales or their next sale. Many will be glad to alert you to upcoming events. Be aware, too, that some stores will give you a refund if you bought at the regular price but the item went on sale just a few weeks later. Some stores, for example, have a thirty-day policy: They will refund the difference between what you paid and the sale price within thirty days, if you bring in your receipt.

Here is a roundup of seasonal sales.

January

AFTER NEW YEAR'S MANY CHRISTMAS ITEMS SELL FOR 75 PERCENT off, including Christmas and holiday cards, decorations, and scented candles. Any candy with Christmas or other holiday packaging can be marked down as much as 75 percent.

Also look for other holiday-related items, that is, products that often sell well as Christmas presents or seasonal items, such as kitchen gadgets, toys, cookware, bathrobes, and slippers.

January is also the end of the winter season for most

stores. This means that they have to get rid of winter merchandise to make way for the spring items. Therefore look for sales on rugs and winter clothing.

Look also for annual white sales of towels, linens, sheets, and other bed-related items. You should also be able to find sales on major appliances and furniture.

February

JUST AS WITH CHRISTMAS, GRAB ANY BOXES OF CANDY WITH Valentine's Day packaging. Expect markdowns as much as 75 percent.

The biggest sales event of February is Presidents' Day, when electronics, audiovisual equipment, and computers often go on sale. Many other businesses may offer Presidents' Day sales as well, such as furniture and mattress stores. You can often find a good deal on air conditioners, exercise equipment, and used cars.

NOTE: The many jewelry sales that seem to pop up just in time for Valentine's Day are often not what they seem. The regular price listed is often highly inflated and the huge sale discount, therefore, not that much of a discount. JCPenney, for example, according to a *New York Times* report in 1992, "inflated its regular jewelry prices with markups as high as five times cost, then advertised discounts up to 60 percent off the regular price to sell the jewelry at what amounted to a typical industry markup." Yet in a court ruling, a judge decided that Penney's practice was not illegal.

March

MARCH TENDS TO BE A QUIETER MONTH FOR SALES BUT LOOK FOR the last of the winter clothes to be on sale (at the very lowest prices of the season) and also promotions for the upcoming spring line of clothing, along with camping and gardening items. Laundry appliances often go on sale in March.

April

EASTER CANDY, ESPECIALLY CHOCOLATE, GETS DRASTICALLY marked down after the holiday. But believe us, chocolate tastes just as good, maybe even better, at up to 75 percent off.

May

IN MAY GARDENING SUPPLIES, LUGGAGE, AND MATTRESSES GO ON sale. Also look for sales on outdoor furniture, TVs, and some appliances, plus sales on spring clothing.

If your schedule allows, May is often a good time to travel at discount prices. Known as a shoulder season (it's not the high season or the low season but in the middle, hence the name), you often will have a more enjoyable time with fewer crowds along with substantial discounts. Since it is just before the peak summer months, you will find most facilities open but prices can be as much as 40 percent less than what you might pay in just another month.

NOTE: Mother's Day jewelry sales may not be what they seem. See our note for February about jewelry sales.

June

LOOK FOR ANNUAL SALES ON ELECTRONICS AND SUMMER SPORTING goods. You may also find sales on furniture and mattresses.

July

THIS MONTH MARKS THE END OF THE SUMMER AND WARM-weather season and stores need to start getting ready for the "back to school" season (the second-busiest season of the year after Christmas). This is a great time to buy a bathing suit and beachwear.

Store-brand clothing often goes on sale at drastic discounts during this time and into August. This is one of the times when you may be able to buy these new clothes below cost.

A number of large items also can go on sale in July. Look for air conditioners, appliances, audiovisual equipment, furniture, bicycles, mattresses, refrigerators, tires, washers, and dryers.

August

THERE ARE VIRTUALLY NO SALES IN AUGUST (EXCEPT AS NOTED FOR July) since there will be a major clearance after Labor Day in September.

September

WARM-WEATHER CLOTHING THAT'S STILL LEFT GETS DUMPED AFTER Labor Day. Look for final clearance (not sales) events on summer and warm-weather products such as summer and spring clothing, camping equipment, outdoor cookware, fans, patio and pool items, and recreational stuff.

There are many new car sales and clearance events from September to the end of the year. But don't buy until the next year's models have been introduced, called the "new model introduction" (NMI), which will give you another 5 percent discount or so. See more about this in our auto section.

Just as in May, the September shoulder season for travel (just after the peak season) is often a good bargain and less crowded.

October

LOOK FOR HALLOWEEN CANDY AT UP TO 75 PERCENT OFF. ALSO look for sales on school items or clearance on back-to-school items.

New cars will be on sale in October. See our explanation about buying after the NMI (in the September section) for the very best deal.

In some areas October is a great time to travel. It is an especially good time to go to Florida, since tourist areas are often a good bargain and less crowded.

November

ODDLY, TURKEYS ARE OFTEN AT THEIR LOWEST COST IN NOVEMBER. Stock up. Put one or two in the freezer.

Look for sales on shoes, used cars, and appliances.

Like October, November also is a great time to go to Florida.

December

DON'T BUY ANYTHING BETWEEN THANKSGIVING AND CHRISTMAS.

Look for some sales immediately after Christmas; the most substantial discounts will be in early January.

#8 SHOPPING TIP #8: UNDERSTAND THE DIFFERENCE BETWEEN A "QUOTE" AND AN "ESTIMATE"

WHEN HAVING WORK DONE ON YOUR CAR OR COMPUTER OR THE like, you should ask for a "quote" rather than an "estimate." A friend of Rick's named Walter Newton, who runs a factory in Durham, North Carolina, gave us this tip: "An estimate is not a quote." Sounds simple, and it is.

What Walter means is that when you ask for a ballpark figure for, say, a car repair (an estimate), don't be surprised when the cost of the repair goes 50 percent above that figure. However, when you ask for a quote, you are asking for a firm dollar amount. And for a quote to have any meaning, you should get it on paper from an authorized employee—preferably an owner or manager—with the job to be done spelled out along with the parts required for the repair. This quote then locks the shop into a set price for a very specific job.

Now, to be realistic a quote works only when a job is fairly straightforward. For example, if you are having an auto repair shop replace a water pump in your car, you should be able to get a firm quote on what that job will cost—although you might add a bit of wiggle room, just in case a hose or two needs to be replaced as well. So you might allow the shop to go a bit over the quote if something more needs to be done.

However, if you bring in a car to a repair shop but are unsure of what is ailing your sputtering engine, asking for a quote would not be possible, since you do not understand what work needs to be done.

The same kind of logic holds for home repair. As Charlie

Boardman, a contractor in Beaufort, North Carolina, said, "new construction can be priced quite accurately," so for new construction get a quote. However, he added, "doing home repair in an older home is often unpredictable," so in this case the buyer will have to live with a rough estimate.

SHOPPING TIP #9: BEWARE THE "MONEY-BACK GUARANTEE" SCAM

THE AS-SEEN-ON-TV "POWERPURIFY" PRODUCT OFFERS A FULL money-back guarantee, but less shipping and handling, and therein lies the scam. In this case shipping and handling, or S&H, is $6.95—almost half the cost of a $15.95 product. This means that to get your money back, you would have to find all your paperwork, write a letter, package the item, insure the package, and then wait for your refund of $15.95, while forfeiting the $6.95 shipping.

We have looked carefully at a number of such as-seen-on-TV ads and many offer about the same thing. A product in the $15–20 range may have an S&H charge that is spelled out in small letters that are hard to read but is about $7. Of course, most people don't return the product, and the company gets to keep the money for something the consumer is not happy with.

Often the voice in the ad tells you in clear language that the offer is "risk-free" because it comes with that money-back guarantee. Yet this means that your "risk-free" purchase cost you about $7, which is a scam in any language. Watch out!

10 SHOPPING TIP #10: BEWARE BOGUS SALES

THERE ARE A NUMBER OF BUSINESSES THAT TRY TO FOOL CONSUMERS into thinking that items are on sale when in fact they are not. For example, some clothing shops will have bogus tags that claim to show that the price has been marked down several times, but that are really sales gimmicks. Furniture stores are famous for doing much the same.

To know if a sale is really a sale, keep in mind the following:

The word *sale* has a specific legal meaning. A sale is a temporary discount from the regular price. After the sale, the price will go back to the normal price.

The words *clearance* or *closeout* are different: These words

People assume items here are on sale, but they're often not, as in the case of this soda. A sale price will be posted if the product is on sale.

are specific and mean that an item will no longer be carried by the store (for at least that season) and that the price will not go back to the regular price. In fact most of these items will continue to drop in price until they are sold, since the store wants to get rid of them and use that money to buy other products that the store can sell more quickly.

If you see signs with "special deal" or "value offer" or other such phrases, you should realize that the words are meaningless. At this point it is up to you to comparison shop, since these words do not indicate that the products are on sale or on clearance.

SHOPPING TIP #11:
DON'T BUY WHAT YOU DON'T NEED

MARKETERS ARE ALWAYS TRYING TO MAKE US LIVE BEYOND OUR needs. According to a study by Charles F. Adams, working with academic researchers Bauer and Greyser, every American is exposed to 560 ads a day, or over 200,000 ads a year (and this is a very, very conservative estimate). In an average lifetime, then, an American will see about 15 million ads. The cumulative effect of all these advertisements is to make you want more than you have and also to be somewhat discontented with your life. After all, the point of ads is to make you a little dissatisfied so you will go out and buy something that will help you be happier and more confident. So how do you avoid the trap of feeling unsatisfied after the drumbeat of 200,000 ads a year? How do you keep from buying things you could live without? Simply be aware of the nature of ads and don't buy things you don't need and never buy to impress someone else.

Over the course of your life it could pay big dividends.

#12 SHOPPING TIP #12:
BEWARE SUGGESTIVE SELLING!

WHEN YOU GO INTO A STORE TO BUY SOMETHING, OR A RESTAURANT to have a bite, if the help has been trained properly you will be the target of suggestive selling techniques. The store or restaurant figures that once you're spending some money, they will help you spend more. And help is the way that suggestive selling is disguised. They don't say, "Do you want to buy something extra?" Instead they will:

1. Suggest additional sales to a customer related to the purchase being made.
2. Suggest an add-on sale that costs less than the principal purchase.
3. Not suggest an add-on until the customer has made a commitment to buy, nor use suggestive selling until after the customer has completed a purchase. In other words the salespeople will approach the customer when she has made a firm decision to buy and her wallet is still open.
4. Not suggest more than a few things, since this will appear to be pushy.

So at a clothing store a "helpful" saleswoman might suggest a scarf to go with a blouse or a belt to go with a pair of pants. At an electronics store the salesman might remind you to buy batteries with the gizmo you are getting. At an audio-video store, a salesperson might encourage you to get an extended warranty. If you're in a restaurant, a waitress might suggest an additional soda or a dessert.

As Rufus Mudsucker, a rent-to-own salesman, points out

in his article "Do You Want Slaw with That?," "It doesn't matter if it's chicken or Cadillacs, son. If you ever expect to sell anything, you've got to ask for it."

Suggestive selling is very important to businesses. For example, *BusinessWeek* reported in November 2005 that Circuit City made most of its profit from the sale of extended warranties (most often sold using suggestive selling) and not the major electronics products themselves.

Salesmen Are Always Trying to Sell You More

*B*enjamin Cheever's book *Selling Ben Cheever* gets to the heart of what selling is all about today. When Cheever was selling computers and electronics, he was taught that "a clerk sells a customer what he or she had intended to buy for what he or she had intended to pay. A salesman, on the other hand, sells the customer more than he or she meant to buy, for more than he or she had expected to pay. A home run . . . meant not only the sale of the highest-priced product possible, but also the accessories, the insurance, and the store credit card."

SHOPPING TIP #13:
BE AWARE OF "UPSELLING"

CLOSELY RELATED TO SUGGESTIVE SELLING IS UPSELLING, WHERE salespeople push you to buy a version of what you want that costs more money, and they certainly have enough versions to sell you. For example, the Lowe's home improvement website lists over seven hundred refrigerators from about $80 to over $8,000 (that's not a typo!). The difference in cost at the low end is about $30 to $50; in other words there is just a modest price increase from one model to the next one up. And with such a small increase in price, salespeople will try to convince you to shell out just a few more dollars than you planned for a model they claim is better.

While manufacturers claim that they offer so many models to give consumers a choice, there is another hidden, more sinister motive. They know that if you come into a store planning on spending $500 on a refrigerator, chances are the trained sales staff can get you to spend 15 to 20 percent more—or in this case about $600. After all, it's just one slight step up—only a bit more than you budgeted for; certainly anyone can afford that. And besides, look at what you will be getting—it's so much better for so little extra money. Well, you get the idea.

SHOPPING TIP #14: BEWARE STORE TRAPS AND IMPULSE BUYING

- *Impulse shopping costs hundreds of dollars each year.*

AS DETAILED IN THIS BOOK, THE SUPERMARKET IS ONE KIND OF store where traps are placed for the unwary and ultimately separate you from your money. For example, that is why you often have to walk to the back of a store to get a quart of milk, past all those other products that you can't help but see as you go by them, and so will possibly buy on impulse. That is why you must walk the entire length of a drugstore to get a prescription filled. Or why stores like Home Depot make you walk through the paint department to get to the wallpaper and blind departments. None of this happens by accident. It is carefully planned, intended to slow you down and get you to spend.

The National Association of Chain Drug Stores and the American Greetings Research Council (NACDS/AG) wanted to find out if drugstores could successfully sell candy at the pharmacy checkout counter without customers being given "the mixed messages suggested by an assortment of chocolate and other confectionery items at the pharmacy counter, which is perceived by consumers as a health care destination," wrote Rob Eder in *Drug Store News*. According to Eder, "there is no arguing with the results of the NACDS/AG research. Countertop displays of chocolate candy placed at the pharmacy counter generated a 32 percent sales impact in the council's tests." "These results were overwhelmingly positive," the NACDS/AG council noted gleefully in its report. "And perhaps most important, the product was sold at full price, so the sales increase also generated a 32 percent increase in profits."

The checkout area is where supermarkets set one of a number of traps for unwary shoppers to entice them to buy candy, magazines, and all kinds of things, including little toys for your kids. This section of the store sells more per square foot than any other part.

If you have a credit card you will be especially vulnerable, because as we mention in this book, you are much more likely to overspend with a credit card. Stores know people can spend impulsively, and they try to make that easy for you!

The bottom line is that you can save a ton by *not buying* on impulse. To resist the siren song of impulse buying, just repeat the old refrain from the "War on Drugs" campaign of the 1980s: "Just say no." Consider it to be a "War on Impulse Buying."

SHOPPING TIP #15: BEWARE PRODUCT PLACEMENT IN MOVIES AND ON TV

ANOTHER INFLUENCE ON CONSUMER BUYING IS A PRACTICE CALLED "product placement," where by moviemakers and TV producers let products appear onscreen to subtly influence our buying decisions. You have probably noticed a logo here and a bottle of vodka there (think *Sex and the City*) and not thought much about it, but over the last twenty years it has become a major marketing tool. Brands worldwide spent $3.07 billion in 2006 for product placements, up from $2.21 billion the year before, according to an article in *Forbes*. For example, the James Bond movie *Die Another Day* featured "Samsonite luggage, Omega watches, a Phillips heart rate monitor, Bollinger champagne, Heineken beer, Sony security systems, laptops, TV cameras and cellphones, and British Airways," the Media Awareness Network of Canada reported. And "according to *Variety*, the movie studio enlisted more than 20 marketing partners who are reportedly contributing at least $100 million in promotional support," wrote Jane Weaver of MSNBC.

Both adults and kids are targets. In Steven Spielberg's movie *E.T.*, the alien E.T.'s fondness for Reese's Pieces caused sales to jump 65 percent. Yet rather than condemning such practices, *BusinessWeek* listed this wildly successful candy placement in their "Placement Hall of Fame" in 1998.

Advertisers love product placement for a number of reasons:

1. They don't appear to be ads, so you, the viewer, are caught unaware.
2. The ads are part of the program, so you can't tune them out or take a break to escape them.

3. These ads are DVR-proof. DVRs can skip over regular ads very quickly, but if the ads are part of the story, you probably won't hit the fast-forward button.
4. They can put them on pay channels, such as HBO.
5. Consumers associate products with admired characters and buy because they like the characters.

SHOPPING TIP #16: MISCELLANEOUS SHOPPING AND BUYING STRATEGIES

THERE ARE A VARIETY OF OTHER SHOPPING STRATEGIES THAT YOU should be aware of so you don't get blindsided by sellers. Don't buy unless you can fairly compare a product or service to another, beware deceptive sales practices, and don't buy something just because it has great quality: you may not need or want to pay for a deluxe product.

Know Where the Discount Shelves Are?

It's a little-known secret, but virtually every store has a clearance section. A big store such as Wal-Mart may have a number of clearance areas, one for each department. Stores like the Gap have closeout bins in the back. If you like to shop, you can save a considerable amount of money by looking at the lowest-priced items first in the closeout areas. Odds are that if you sort through the discount bins, you'll find something at a good price, such as clothes that look just as good as something else that costs full price.

DON'T BUY UNLESS YOU CAN COMPARISON SHOP

Hidden costs, such as bank fees and airline surcharges, are an annoying part of modern marketing. But beyond the annoyance factor is an even more troublesome aspect. Our free market society is based on the assumption that a consumer can comparison shop and after doing so pick the best mousetrap for the lowest price.

However, modern marketing is designed to prevent comparison shopping, since these dozens of hidden fees are not obvious. This makes it virtually impossible to find the cost of using one bank service compared to another, for example.

For this reason, we recommend that you do your best to keep it simple whenever possible. For example, a long-distance service with a flat per-minute rate is much easier to understand and use than one with different pricing for the time of day (see our telephone chapter). A low-priced airline flight is better than a higher-priced one with frequent-flier miles that might expire or be devalued.

Southwest Airlines Ad Reveals Hidden Pricing

*I*n an ad by Southwest Airlines in *USA Today*, the company claims that other airlines tack on an additional $77 worth of hidden fees (on average) to the cost of flying. So while Southwest might charge $69 for a flight, another airline with hidden fees actually charges $146 for the same flight. However, this may not be obvious since these hidden fees are . ∴. well . . . hidden.

DON'T BUY SUPERIOR QUALITY IF YOU DON'T NEED IT

The ads for many everyday brand-name products are impressive. The Bounty "quicker picker upper" will soak up more spilled coffee and do it faster than a store-brand towel—and we don't doubt the ad. It can also be rinsed out and reused while a store-brand towel will disintegrate. Again, we won't argue the point.

Then there is Reynolds Wrap aluminum foil that is stronger than the store-brand stuff. As the Reynolds Wrap website says, "No matter how tough the situation, use Reynolds Wrap® Foil to get professional results every time you fire up the grill." And there are Glad ForceFlex trash bags, which will hold a broken piano (now we assume this is an exaggeration, but the point is the bag is strong). We know that you've heard the sales pitch for these super name-brand items at every turn—from Ziploc storage bags to Charmin toilet paper.

Again, we are not disputing the claims of these products. However, we have to ask one important question: Do you really need a plastic garbage bag that will hold a broken piano? We think it is unlikely. If you need a quicker picker upper for spilled coffee, use two store-brand towels. Or if you are worried that your cheaper aluminum foil is not strong enough for one of the foods on your grill, use two sheets.

While this might seem a bit silly, the point is still the same one we have been making throughout this book. You are being sold a capability that you don't really need and paying a lot extra for that.

But of course, by all means, if you do need the capability, if you do need the "quicker picker upper" because your two-year-old spills juice on a hourly basis, that is a solid buying decision—just don't buy it because you "might" need it occasionally.

IS A DISCOUNT CARD WORTH THE MONEY?

Is it just another marketing trick, or can discount cards that you pay for save you real money? Just do a little math and you'll know the answer sooner than you can say, "Lend me your calculator for a minute."

At a bookstore, Rick was offered a discount card by Books-A-Million that would save him money for a year and was good at any Books-A-Million store. The cost of the card was $15 and the discount was 10 percent off everything in the store, even books that were already discounted or on sale. Hmm, seemed like a good idea, but why not do a little math?

Before buying a card like this, decide what the break-even point for the card is—that is, the point where the saved discount based on the amount of money you spend will pay for the cost of the card. By doing this you can decide if it is likely that you will at least have gotten enough discounts to pay for the initial price of the card.

The math for this particular card is simple. Divide the discount percentage into the full price, which is 100 percent. Then multiply that times the price of the card. In this case $100/10 = 10$, and $10 \times \$15$ (the cost of the card) = $150. So Rick would have to buy at least $150 worth of stuff from a Books-A-Million store in the next year to break even.

To take a more complicated example, suppose you got a 15 percent discount on a cup of coffee for a year if you bought a discount card for $20. How much money would you have to spend at the coffee shop to break even? $100/15 = 6.66$. Then $6.66 \times \$20$ (the price of the card) = $133.33 worth of coffee, the break-even point. A good rule of thumb is that if you think there is a remote chance that you will not reach the break-even point, don't bother. Why pay money up front for a discount that might not save you money?

So in the case of Books-A-Million, Rick decided it was not worth it, since he didn't do that much business with Books-A-Million stores during a year.

PART
2.

Insiders' Tips for
Saving Money on
Specific Products
and Services

Chapter 1

AUTOMOBILE EXPENSES

🛒

*Y*ou can dramatically cut your costs across the board so that owning a car doesn't eat up your paycheck. From getting better gas mileage, to repairs, to insurance, to buying a new or used car, we'll show you lots of ways to pay less.

CUTTING THE COST OF GAS

DON'T USE GAS-SAVING GADGETS

Gas-saving gadgets? Steer clear! Be skeptical about any gizmo that promises to improve gas mileage. The Environmental Protection Agency (EPA) has tested more than one hundred supposed gas-saving devices, including "mixture enhancers" and fuel line magnets, and found that very few provided any benefits. Those devices that did work provided only a slight improvement. Some products do work—in reverse, damaging your car's engine or causing a substantial increase in exhaust emissions.

The FTC has an informative site called "Gas Savings Products? Fact or Fuelishness," at www.ftc.gov/bcp/edu/pubs/consumer/autos/aut10.shtm.

BE AWARE OF ZONE PRICING AND SAVE 10 PERCENT

In 2005, staff writers Elizabeth Douglass and Gary Cohn of the *Los Angeles Times* warned about something called "zone pricing." The practice continues today, and it can cost you heavily. For example, on the same day in mid-June 2008, Mobil regular gas was selling for $4.89 a gallon in one Los Angeles neighborhood, and for $4.39 a gallon in another L.A. neighborhood—a half-dollar difference. The zone pricing difference is just another dirty little secret of oil companies. No oil company is going to tell you exactly how zone pricing works, but it seems to be a formula based on traffic patterns, location, and the economic stratum of the neighborhood. (Ever notice how run-down neighborhoods have higher-priced gas?) It can be surprising. Rick once noticed a 5 percent difference in the same brand and grade of gas at stations that were a scant two blocks from each other in Greenville, North Carolina.

All you have to do to take advantage of zone pricing is to get in the habit of keeping it at the front of your mind. Then, while traveling your normal routes, keep an eye out for the station that has the lowest price. You can also look on the Internet for the best daily prices, using sites such as www.gasbuddy.com. The cheapest gas may be close enough to justify a trip there. Of course, if gas is 40 cents cheaper in Guam but you live in Minneapolis, forget it!

Don't Rock the Pedal

*A*t one point in his illustrious career, Tom was driving a limo to make ends meet, and one day when he came back from taking someone to the airport, his boss called him over and told Tom that people liked him as a driver except for one thing: he rode the gas pedal as if it were the pedal on a sewing machine. That's a good way to drive if you want to waste gas.

USE CRUISE CONTROL

A couple of mechanics we know say that when it comes to saving gas, using cruise control can be quite an asset. According to Jack Danahy, a mechanic in Lake Ronkonkoma, Long Island, "Gas gets wasted when the driver goes up and down on the pedal. Using cruise control stabilizes the use." But while it is good on flat roads, Danahy suggests that you flip the switch back out of cruise control when going up or down hills. "Here," he said, "it can be dangerous. You want to be in total control of the speed."

How much gas can cruise control save? Danahy says simply, "A lot!" A test by Edmunds (www.edmunds.com) found that it can save you up to 14 percent.

NO ADVANTAGE TO USING PREMIUM GAS

You've seen the ads and probably been tempted every time you fill up at a gas station. Premium gas will keep your car running better, longer, with more power—right? For example, Shell makes a highly promoted "V-Power" premium gasoline that the company claims "actively cleans for better performance." The company further claims, "Shell V-Power was carefully designed to be safe and effective for use in all vehicles." And after all, doesn't your car deserve premium gas? However, this is all nonsense. The Federal Trade Commission (FTC) has stated that "in most cases, using a higher-octane gasoline than your owner's manual recommends offers absolutely no benefit. It won't make your car perform better, go faster, get better mileage or run cleaner." The FTC went on to say, "Studies indicate that altogether, drivers may be spending hundreds of millions of dollars each year for higher octane gas than they need." Of course it does make gasoline company executives feel better. Premium gas is designed for a specific engine that can take advantage of the gas's qualities—qualities that are wasted in a normal engine—and it may cause an engine designed for regular gas to actually have less power and get lower mileage. (That also may make gas execs happier.) Moreover, there is evidence that running premium gas in your car may be harmful to the environment. For example, say the NPR *Car Talk* guys, "most experts say excess octane creates more pollution."

The only way to know for sure which gas your car should run on is to look in your owner's manual. Sometimes the required gas grade is indicated on your car, such as on the gas cap or close to the point where you fill the tank. The only possible benefit to Shell's V-Power gas is that it has more than the government-mandated amount of detergents. However, you can buy a more potent cleaning solution that you simply add to a tank of gas every couple of months. Among these are the products made by Gumout, and they cost much less.

OTHER WAYS TO REDUCE GAS USE: ELEVEN TIPS

NOTE: Tom did his own study of various ways to increase your gas mileage. Here is his report:

1. Get That "Check Engine" Light Checked Out
Possible savings: Off the charts

A faulty oxygen sensor—a fairly common cause of those unexplained "check engine" lights—can actually cost you up to 40 percent of your engine's performance. If the light's on, make the appointment now. It could pay for itself very quickly.

2. Check Your Tire Pressure

Possible savings: 133.9 gallons/year. Obama was right!

According to some government estimates, the average driver can boost fuel efficiency 10 percent just by keeping tires properly inflated. That's often a free, or cheap, repair. On my way to work, I pass two gas stations with air compressors I can use for free, and three—apparently owned by cheapskates—that take quarters.

3. Change Your Air Filter

Possible savings: 60.9 gallons/year

Gas is half the combustion equation. Air is the other half. A clogged air filter can rob 10 percent of your engine's efficiency. A new air filter can get that 10 percent back—usually for under $15.

4. Drive 60 on the Highway, Not 75

Possible savings: 57.8 gallons/year

On the highway, stay close to the speed limit, and keep your speed as constant as traffic allows. Most cars reach optimal gas mileage at about 60 miles per hour. Speeding up increases wind resistance against the car, making the engine work harder and burn more gas. According to the EPA, each 5 miles per hour over 60 that you drive decreases fuel efficiency by up to 7 percent.

5. Turn off the AC

Possible savings: 31.9 gallons/year

Some air conditioners rob an engine up to 5 percent of its fuel economy.

There is some controversy about this one: Many newer cars are able to compensate for the energy used by an air conditioner and don't suffer the same penalty for keeping you cool.

6. Get Your Engine Tuned
Possible savings: 25.8 gallons/year

Most of us can boost our gas mileage by 4 percent with a simple tune-up. And when you get a tune-up, have the mechanic check that the fuel injection is working properly. Poor fuel injection can be very costly.

7. Drive Calmly in the City
Possible savings: 17.9 gallons/year

There's a red light up ahead. You're going to stop when you get to it. Do you keep your foot on the gas until it's time to brake for the light? Most of us do, but that doesn't necessarily make sense. The EPA estimates that accelerating rapidly and braking hard can reduce your car's fuel efficiency by as much as 5 percent. And that may be a low estimate. Look at it this way—are you willing to spend money to stop at that light sooner?

8. Lose Weight in Your Trunk
Possible savings: 13.1 gallons/year for each hundred pounds you remove

Government estimates say that an extra hundred pounds in your car can reduce fuel efficiency by up to 2 percent. And that's an average—the smaller the car, the more that extra weight makes the engine work harder. So empty the trunk. And in winter, don't just scrape the windshield, scrape the entire car—snow and ice add to the weight of your car.

9. Lose the Roof Rack
Possible savings: 13.1 gallons/year

Wind resistance is the enemy of fuel efficiency. Do you have a roof rack? Every time you drive, it's making your car fight wind resistance, and burn fuel. Most of the time, that's money you're spending to carry an empty roof rack. Get a 2 percent boost by taking the thing off.

10. Change Your Oil on Time
Possible savings: 6.6 gallons/year

After three thousand miles, changing your oil (using the recommended grade) gives you back 1 percent of your car's miles-per-gallon rating.

11. Check Your Gas Cap
Possible savings: 10 gallons/year

The Consumer Federation of America "estimates that nearly 17 percent of cars on the road today have broken or missing gas caps." This means that gas is evaporating into the air, which is costing you money. Replacing a bad cap could save you 3 cents a gallon. And in the same vein, make sure that, even if you have a cap in good working order, you always tighten your gas cap so that no vapors escape.

HOW MUCH GAS COULD YOU SAVE?

If you follow the eleven gas-saving tips above, you could be spending about $1,500 less on gas in the next year (at an estimated $4 a gallon). Though it's a rough estimate, it shows you what small changes in your habits—most of which you can make for free—could do for your wallet.

REPAIRS AND MAINTENANCE

BEWARE MECHANICS WHO ONLY CHANGE PARTS

You go to a repair shop because your car is overheating. After three days without a car and then a $400 bill, you are finally back on the road. But guess what? Your car is still overheating. You take the car back and the shop can prove that it replaced the parts it claims to have replaced and that it wasn't trying to rip you off. But you are stuck. You leave the car for another three days and another $400, all the while feeling that something is very wrong. There's a name for this kind of repair shop, a name known to professionals who work with cars: these shops are called "parts changers."

These guys don't know how to properly diagnose a car. So they simply install new parts. After all, they have nothing to lose. It might fix the problem and it might not. So while the shop can document that it did the work, it will make money each time it installs a new part (one that you may not have needed).

SOLUTION

Ask your friends and colleagues about repair shops that fix a car right the first time. And when you take a car in for repair, insist that the mechanics do a thorough diagnostic check before doing any work.

DON'T DIAGNOSE PROBLEMS YOURSELF

We've seen it over and over. A driver limps into a repair shop, jumps out of the car, says that a specific gizmo in his vehicle is not working, and leaves the car for repairs. But guess what? The gizmo was not the problem. So now the driver is stuck with paying the bill—after all, he told the repair shop exactly what to fix—and the car is still broken. The solution is simple. Unless you are a mechanic, don't diagnose your car's problems. Instead describe the symptoms to the mechanic and then let the repair shop figure out what is wrong. For example, if your car does not have as much power as it used to, don't tell the shop to replace fuel injection components. Instead tell the shop that it seems to have power on a straightaway but not when climbing hills. Then let the shop diagnose the problem.

DON'T BUY TIRES THAT ARE OUT OF DATE

- *Tires over six years old are capable of catastrophic failure.*

About five years ago, Rick was driving madly down the highway, fleeing an approaching hurricane, when suddenly he heard a loud sound. He pulled to the side of the road and found that the tread had completely come off his tire and all that was left was the bare core. Apparently he had a tire that was too old and the tread had simply separated. But he was one of the lucky ones. ABC's 20/20 reported in May 2008 that a number of people have been injured or even killed when old tires come apart on the highway.

The tire industry doesn't want you to know about this. It's generally agreed that tires begin to degrade after about six years. Yet tires that are six years old and older are being sold as new in the United States. In Europe, tires that are out of date (meaning six years old or more), as they often are in the United States, would be illegal.

The National Highway Traffic Safety Administration (NHTSA, a division of the U.S. Department of Transportation) said in a June 2008 press release, "Old tires . . . are subject to greater stress, which increases the likelihood of catastrophic failure."

The NHTSA also pointed out, "The age of the tire can be determined by checking the identification number on the sidewall that begins with the letters 'DOT.' The last four digits represent the week and year the tire was manufactured."

Bottom line: Protect your car, your family, and yourself when buying a new tire. Always check the date the tire was made and refuse to buy a tire that is older than six years.

GET AN OWNER'S MANUAL!

After taking ownership of your car, buy the owner's manual if the car didn't come with one. In these days of the Internet and eBay, finding an owner's manual is not very hard. Simply search for the make and model of the car you own. While you may have to pay a bit of a premium price, the cost is well worth it, as you will probably save many times that amount. For example, Rick had an owner's manual for his old Buick. When the security light came on and would not go off, the car wouldn't start. He didn't know what had happened and worried that he would need to take it to a repair shop and spend hundreds of dollars. Instead he pulled out the owner's manual, which told him that the security system had been triggered and that if he waited seven minutes, it would reset itself and the car would start, which it did.

BUYING A CAR

THE BEST DEAL IS USUALLY A LATE-MODEL USED CAR

Car ads scream at us from the TV. Get the latest, the greatest— get rid of that old clunker and be the envy of your neighborhood. The implication: You are a worthless swine who will be ennobled and uplifted by a new car. Furthermore, who wouldn't like to own a new car? We can all fantasize about that wonderful new-car smell and the peace of mind that comes with knowing you won't need repairs for a very long time.

So what's wrong with this picture?

The problem with new cars is very simple: They have no repair history. Manufacturers change their designs all the time, and so when you buy a new car, you have no idea whether it has a lot of bugs or is trouble free or is related to a component in lemonade. Even if it comes with a good warranty, who wants to keep taking their car to the shop?

A used car does have a history. A one- or two-year-old model may have been reported on by tens of thousands of consumers who have driven the auto firsthand. So if you buy a late-model car with an excellent repair history, you know what you are getting. In addition, you will have saved as much as 30 percent over the price of a new car. In addition you will have saved on sales tax, insurance costs, and property tax.

The *Car Talk* guys of NPR have said, "From a purely financial point of view, there is no question that buying a used car is always cheaper, even in the long run." We believe that the best deal by far is a late-model auto, from two to five years old. And this car will often be more reliable and require fewer repairs than a new car bought off the dealer's lot.

So how do you know that you are getting a great deal? Find back issues of the *Consumer Reports Annual Buying Guide* at your local library and look through the very detailed repair reports at the back of the book. These statistics are based on thousands of reports from car owners covering an eight-year period. The reports cover virtually every aspect of a car's reliability, with sixteen categories in all. After studying the data, select a used car, truck, or van that has lower-than-average problems in most areas and does not have any higher-than-average components that cause trouble.

WAIT TO BUY A CAR, GAIN ANOTHER 5 PERCENT

- *Don't buy during fall sales, but a bit later, after the new model introduction (NMI).*

Hurry, hurry, get your best deals of the year in the fall when the models are about to change—right? Wrong! Car dealers try to rid their lots of cars before next year's autos come out but the very best deals are *after* the new models are on the showroom floor, known in the trade as the new model introduction (NMI).

Once the new models are out, those new cars (which had been on clearance) are now last year's cars—and this means that you can save another 5 percent. While this may not sound like a lot, for a $20,000 car this adds up to $1,000 off the price, for example.

Buys the Car Sight Unseen!

Barbara Brown of New Bern, North Carolina, uses Edmunds (www.edmunds.com), which shows what all types of cars are generally selling for. This determines what she'll pay for a new car. Intellichoice (www.intellichoice.com) and the Kelley Blue Book (www.kbb.com) are other good sites. She then sends that price to a number of dealers and tells them to contact her only if they will accept that price—period. Dealers have accepted her offers for the last two new cars she has bought. Indeed, in both instances she didn't even see a car salesman until they came to her door with the paperwork, the keys, a big thank-you—and the car.

NEGOTIATE YOUR CAR'S PRICE CORRECTLY

- *Understand the three negotiations that are involved each time you buy a car.*

Let's say you bought a car that you wanted, at the price you wanted. You took the time to compare prices before buying a new or used car from a dealer and you came prepared for the hard bargaining that followed. Yet while you were pretty certain that you paid the right price for your new set of wheels, you couldn't shake that nagging feeling that you paid more than you should have. And if you felt this way, chances are you were right. The problem with buying a car is that it often involves at least three negotiations. The first is for the price of the car you want to buy. The second is for the value of your trade-in. The third is for the financing.

It really pays to do your homework. Know the market value of the car you want. Research the trade-in value of your old car when you sell it to a dealer. And shop around for different loan deals based on the kind of car you are buying. Note that you will pay more on a loan for a used car than for a new car. Also, when you are at the dealer's, insist that each negotiation be separate. Dealers love to mix these three negotiations together almost like a shell game, so that you become a bit bewildered. For example, a dealer might wave a low and tempting monthly payment in front of your nose. And while such a payment might be good for your cash flow, it tells you nothing of the nitty gritty of your deal with the dealer.

Today you needn't go in blind. You can find the value of the car you want to buy and your trade-in value from Edmunds (www.edmunds.com) and Kelley Blue Book (www.kbb.com).

HOW ABOUT A STATE-OF-THE-ART PLUG-IN HYBRID?

- *A plug-in hybrid runs on gas and electricity with battery power and can cost as little as the equivalent of 15 cents a gallon of gas to run.*

"Plug-in" hybrids are the next generation of energy-efficient hybrid cars. Both Toyota (the Prius) and GM (the Volt) have plug-in hybrid autos that they plan to roll out in the near future, most likely by late 2009, in limited quantities. (Please note that GM's hybrid is a very different design from Toyota's, but for our purposes the term *hybrid* still applies.)

If you are unfamiliar with the term, a plug-in hybrid is a car that can be plugged into a house current to charge its batteries. While the batteries will only allow the car to run a short distance just on battery power, this might be enough for most commutes. Once the battery power is used up, the hybrid switches over to its internal engine and runs as a normal hybrid.

The advantage to such a car is that charging the batteries is much cheaper than filling up with gas. And (as the smart readers of this book know) if you charge up these batteries off-peak with a time-of-use (TOU) electrical rate, the cost of charging the batteries can be almost nothing. For example, GM claims the price of charging their Volt hybrid would be like paying 60 cents a gallon for gas; if recharging were done at night at the TOU rate, the cost could run as low as 15 cents a gallon!

Also, some of these new hybrids may qualify for a federal tax credit.

HIRE A NEGOTIATOR? HOW TO GET A $10,000 CAR FOR $2,800

Rick's wife bought a two-year-old Chrysler minivan with a book value of over $10,000 for $2,800. While this sounds too good to be true, the deal came with some conditions. First, she found an experienced man who went to car auctions and was a trusted friend of a close friend. Next, Rick's wife had a limited choice about what kind of car she could get. About all she could specify was that she wanted a late-model minivan for about $3,000. She could not pick the color or the year or even the make or model. At a car auction about a month later, the car buyer found a minivan that matched what she wanted and made the deal. And at that point Rick's wife was committed to buying what the buyer had chosen.

She has had the car for three years and has been delighted. It's another example of how you can live very well if you are willing to be a bit flexible.

Back-Door Discount

Jane and Roy Stillwell, a young couple from Miami, Oklahoma, found exactly the used car they wanted, and tried to convince the mechanic who was selling it to let it go for a lower price. He wouldn't budge. Still, they figured that the price was reasonable and therefore decided to buy it. "However," said Roy, "we asked the mechanic if he would put on four new tires at his cost, which he agreed to do. So while he would not come down on the overall price, we still got a discount."

HOW MUCH DOES A CAR REALLY COST TO OPERATE?

If you want to know exactly what owning a particular new car will cost before plunking down your hard-earned cash, use Edmunds True Cost to Own calculator (www.edmunds.com). Just input the make, model, and year.

BEWARE "OPPORTUNITY PRICING"

In a new and very deceptive marketing ploy, some companies are using a tactic called "opportunity pricing" to entice consumers, especially low-income consumers. This tactic involves getting the consumers to reveal how much they earn and also what their household expenses are. The price of a used car, for example, along with the financing is then adjusted to fit their budget. Prices of the cars on the lot are never displayed.

In other words, the price of the car is determined by the seller, based on the income of the customer—thus the term *opportunity pricing*. Naturally a car bought in this manner will generally cost a lot more than it should—and the same is true with higher financing expenses. Companies that employ this kind of tactic justify it by saying they are offering cars and other products to people with poor credit—cars and products that they could not otherwise afford.

Opportunity pricing also reveals why you should never tell a car salesman, for example, what your monthly salary is or how much a month you can afford. A smart salesman will then adjust the price of a car or the financing offer to fit your income—and in that case you are almost certain to come out a loser.

Turned into Bette Davis

*O*ne woman (name withheld) turned into Bette Davis to buy a car cheaper. She had been to a used car place and was interested in an SUV that was selling for $3,700. She had her mechanic check it out and he said it was in excellent shape and worth $450–$700 more than its sale price. She went back to the dealer and with a somewhat flat, resigned voice—and expression—said, "I took it to a mechanic. After he looked it over, I decided I can give you $3,000." The dealer took her money— and never bothered to ask what dire problems the mechanic found. In our experience most used car dealers or, excuse us, pre-owned dealers, don't know in any detail what shape the cars in their lot are in. They have cars flowing in from every- where and simply can't know everything about all of them.

LEASING

THINK TWICE BEFORE YOU LEASE A CAR

- *At the end of a lease you own nothing.*

Should you lease a car, or buy one? The answer is simple: After being locked into a multiyear lease and making all the pay- ments and doing the required regular maintenance, you have nothing to show for it. In 1997 Rick Doble interviewed Leslie Byrne, who was the director of what was then named the U.S. Office of Consumer Affairs, about car leases. She responded, "When you have paid off a car loan, you own the car. When you have paid off the lease, you own nothing." She went even fur- ther and told Rick that she had asked a car dealer what a con- sumer owned at the end of the lease period. The dealer replied, "The possibility of equity." In other words, nothing.

Buy Your Leased Gas-Guzzling SUV

*I*f you already drive a leased SUV and can live with the gas mileage, consider this: At the end of your lease, you may be able to get a sweet deal if you want to buy your SUV. Now that the price of these vehicles has dropped as much as 60 percent after three years due to their terrible gas mileage (instead of the normal 30–40 percent), you should be able to buy yours at a very favorable price. Dealers will bargain with you because they won't want another used SUV sitting on their lot, going unsold.

AUTOMOBILE INSURANCE

FAST, EASY COMPARISON SHOPPING FOR CAR INSURANCE

- *Get unbiased government car insurance cost comparison information for your area.*

Everyone knows that they should compare prices for auto insurance, but it seems like a lot of work. You could call a few companies, give them a ton of personal information such as your age, the make and year of your car, your driving record, the type of driving you'll be doing, etc., and then get some prices. After that you can expect to get annoying phone calls from an agent wanting to sell you a policy. Most people just give up and go with a company they are familiar with, which is of course what your insurance company is hoping you will do.

There has to be a simpler way! And believe it or not, there is. It's a method that could save you hundreds of dollars each year. As we mention under homeowner's insurance, your state's insurance department often has comprehensive price comparisons for different insurers in different parts of the state. With auto insurance these departments use a standard driver profile as a basis for comparison.

To show you how this works we'll focus on Arizona as an example. The Arizona Department of Insurance website has an updated comparison guide for auto insurance in different towns in Arizona. For example, rates for a married couple (who drive fifteen miles each way to work, have a clean driving record, and a median credit score and who live in the Tucson) could pay as little as $357 or as much as $4,010 for a policy with the same coverage. This comparison lists over fifty insurers in ten different areas (urban and rural) and includes the number of complaints and a compl aint ratio for each company. To add icing to the cake, there are price comparisons for a number of different typical driver profiles. To make this comparison yourself, be aware that virtually every state has an insurance department and most states, we've found, have these kinds of comparisons online. Visit your state's insurance department, navigate to the consumer division, and then look for a page with automobile insurance comparisons.

EXAMPLE 1

DRIVER: Female age 41. No at-fault accidents or traffic violations during the past three years.
VEHICLE: 2001 Grand Cherokee (Symbol 14)
USE: Drives to work fewer than 15 miles each way and under 15,000 miles a year .

Territory	1	2	5	7	9	20	21	22	23	24	
Allstate	$803 to $876*	$772 to $803*	$814	$803	$785	$866	$772	$902	$906	$906	$8 $8
The Concord Group	$952	$901	$1,108	$1,107	$1,050	$1,007	$931	$1,083	$1,193	$997	$1
Dairyland Insurance Company	$2,976	$2,304	$2,160	$2,244	$2,076	$1,872	$1,968	$2,028	$1,944	$2,652	$2
GEICO	$698	$698	$722.40	$701.80	$703	$727.80	$720.40	$764.40	$771	$776	$7
MMG** Insurance Company	$1,057	$845	$851	$836	$851	$866	$866	$1,057	$953	$927	$7
Patriot Mutual Insurance Company	$829	$829	$813	$775	$813	$852	$829	$901	$893	$893	$7
Patrons Oxford	$745	$675	$766	$748	$766	$755	$723	$816	$838	$779	$7
Peerless	$948	$1,265	$906	$906	$906	$982	$883	$1,120	$1,069	$958	$6
State Farm Mutual	$657.60	$591.60	$602.40	$558	$602.40	$573.60	$551.20	$654	$638.40	$602.80	$5

* Range of premiums represent territories different from those listed.   Please check with individual companies for specific
**Company has different territories than those listed in the chart for Brunswick, Top sham, Yarmouth, Camden, and Rockp
company for specific rates for these cities.

Typical comparison of car insurance policies by a state insurance department.

PROTECTING YOUR CAR

CHEAPER THEFT PROTECTION FOR YOUR CAR

- *Forget expensive car alarms. A kill switch makes a car very hard to steal with no false alarms.*

A great but cheap security trick to prevent someone from stealing your car is a device called an "ignition kill switch," which those funny but very well-informed brothers Tom and Ray of NPR's *Car Talk* say is "the most effective antitheft device. [It] kills power to the ignition, the fuel pump or both." Such a switch—costing around $10 or $20 to install instead of the $100 to $200 for a standard alarm system—can be installed by yourself or by a mechanic in a hidden spot in your car. The thief will try to start your car but it will "crank and crank, and won't start," say Ray and Tom, "and the thief isn't going to take the time to diagnose the problem and figure out why the car isn't starting." One caveat: Before installing an ignition kill switch, check to see if your carmaker allows it. Some don't, and installing it may void the warranty.

Summary: Money-Saving Tips for Automobile Expenses

GAS SAVINGS

- Steer clear of gas-saving gadgets.
- Be aware of zone pricing.
- Use cruise control.
- Be aware of premium gas scam.
- Don't buy tires that are out of date.
- Get the check-engine light checked out.
- Check tire pressure.
- Change air filter.

- Drive 60 on highway, not 75.
- Turn off AC.
- Get engine tuned.
- Drive calmly in city.
- Lose weight in trunk.
- Don't use roof rack.
- Change oil regularly.

REPAIRS

- Beware parts changers.
- Don't diagnose your own car problems.

BUYING A CAR

- Best new-car deals are offered after new models are introduced.
- Buying a used car is usually a better deal than buying a new car.
- Buying a car involves three negotiations (price, trade-in, and financing).

AUTO INSURANCE

- Use your state insurance department website for detailed cost comparisons.

Chapter 2

BANKING

🛒

*T*here are a number of ways to keep more of your money when dealing with banks, but these days one of the main concerns is whether keeping one's money in the bank is safe. The main reason was the collapse of California's IndyMac Bank in July 2008 and Washington Mutual in September 2008, as well as other banks. IndyMac suffered losses—$709 million in the last two quarters of 2007—and its customers began to worry the bank might fail. Then in late June, depositors withdrew $1.3 billion in eleven days. Fearing a bank run, federal regulators transferred control of the bank to the Federal Deposit Insurance Corporation (FDIC). Experts estimate that the failure of IndyMac will cost the FDIC from $4 billion to $8 billion. Depositors lost about $500 million. However, those losses had to do with dollars that were not insured. (Read below about how to make sure your money is 100 percent safe.)

Though the tumult is hardly over, the bottom line is that banks are still the safest place to stash your cash, according to the Better Business Bureau. The FDIC has created an undisclosed list of troubled banks that are at risk of failure. The list was built with some reliance on the "Texas ratio," a formula that compares a bank's assets and reserves to its nonperforming loans. Banks with a ratio over 100 percent are considered the most at risk for failure. Considering there are more than 8,500 banks in the United States, and that only about 1 percent have made the troubled list, the FDIC is advising consumers not to worry about the security of their bank.

HOW TO KEEP YOUR MONEY 100 PERCENT SAFE

To keep your money safe you have to know the rules. And the rules can be quite simple, as easy as one, two, three. Here is what we suggest: First, only put your money in a bank that is protected by the FDIC or in a credit union that is protected by the National Credit Union Administration (NCUA).

According to Eric Solis, a certified financial planner, "The FDIC insures $100,000 *per* depositor *per* insured savings association." This means that if you have a savings account and a CD that add up to $100,000 or less, you are covered. Luckily, in the case of IndyMac, the FDIC has agreed to pay customers 50 percent of the value of their uninsured deposits. If you have more than the insured limit, put money above $100,000 in a different FDIC- or NCUA-protected bank, that is, not a different branch, but a different banking institution. The late 2008 bailout or rescue plan contained a provision for FDIC insurance coverage to increase to $250,000 at all FDIC-insured banks, but this may only be a temporary measure. The betting is that this measure will become permanent or, at the very least, the old $100,000 maximum will be raised—so check with your bank about changes in the FDIC insured deposit limits.

In any case, it's not a good idea to put all your eggs in one basket or all your money (even if insured) in the same bank. In the unlikely event that a bank does fail, and even though your account is totally insured and safe, there might be an interruption in your ability to access those funds. Let's say you have $150,000. To be safe you could put $75,000 in one insured bank and the same amount in another. Having your money in different banks adds an extra measure of safety and almost guarantees that you will always have immediate access to at least one of your accounts, since it is unlikely that two different banks will fail at the same time.

NOTE: Under some conditions you can have much more than $100,000 insured at the same bank, but we wanted to keep it simple. If you want to put more than $100,000 in the same bank, we recommend that you go to the FDIC website and use the Electronic Deposit Insurance Estimator (EDIE), which "allows you to calculate the insurance coverage of your accounts at each FDIC-insured institution," according to the FDIC (www4.fdic.gov/EDIE).

AVOID CHECK-BALANCING MISTAKES

- *A software calculator gives you an electronic "tape"*
  of your calculations and makes balancing easy.

Many people have trouble reconciling their checkbook balance with their bank account statement when they use a standard calculator. When the checkbook and the bank statement do not agree, they need to be able to review and double-check the full list of numbers that they entered. It is very hard to find a mistake when you don't have the complete set of numbers in front of you. Businesses use calculators with printers, but we have seen few electronic calculators with this capability. However, there is a very good software version called ShowCalc. For most household finance chores, the simple free version is available. For more sophisticated work, you may want the paid version. Just use the number pad on your computer keyboard and the calculator will be as easy to use as a handheld model.

ShowCalc—Freeware Version
www.321download.com/LastFreeware/page7.html

ShowCalc—Calculator with a tape ($17.50),
try free for thirty days
www.softpedia.com/get/Others/Home-Education/Showcalc.shtml

BUY CHEAPER CHECKS

When you open a bank account, you are given an initial set of checks, often printed by Deluxe or Harland Clarke. When the time comes to print some more, you might be astonished at the cost. It can be $20 for a box, a price you could buy a hardcover book at. Many people order them because they think that the banks checks are somehow better or safer or more reliable than other checks. Not true. In fact the reason you pay so much is that, as in the case of the former John H. Harland Company, "Checks were a high-profit item for banks and other financial institutions, who marked up the price by 20–30 percent." So still today you are paying a high retail price for checks that are then marked up by your bank.

We recommend that you order from a third-party check printer such as Wal-Mart (www.walmartchecks.com) or Artistic Checks (www.artisticchecks.com). You can save from 50 to 75 percent. While this is not a huge cost, it is one more blow against institutions that overcharge us without giving us any added benefit.

Order Checks Early

*D*on't order third-party checks at the last minute. Order when you have plenty of time, since a new check order, for security reasons, can take a while. "The checks work fine," says Tom's wife, Catherine. "Look for coupons in those coupon flyers you regularly get in the mail. The checks are available in color and a wide variety of designs which you don't pay extra for."

AVOID ATM FEES

It certainly is the height of chutzpah, admits one banker, for you to have to pay a bank to get your hands on your own money. Welcome to the modern world of the ATM. Still, if you need cash but the banks are closed, ATMs are essential. You can avoid some fees, though, as follows:

- Get cash only from your own bank's machine. But make sure you can. For example, Washington Mutual has such a card without a fee, although it can be used only on their ATMs. And keep in mind that the amount you can withdraw daily is less than with a regular credit card. Also note that some banks will charge you even if you use a credit card issued by them.
- When buying groceries at a supermarket, ask the checkout person to charge an extra $20 or $40 more on your check card, which you will then get back as cash, thus saving an ATM fee.
- Use credit union ATMs; some don't charge a fee.

LOWER YOUR BANK FEES

According to research firm SNL Financial, customers paid banks $32 billion in account fees in 2004. There are a couple of ways to fights fees, however. First, consider banking at a large bank with multiple convenient ATMs where there is no charge for withdrawals, which can be up to $4 per transaction. (Double-check to make sure that your bank doesn't charge you.) Then shop around for free checking and make sure you don't violate the conditions of the free checks, such as keeping a minimum balance so you don't pay monthly fees. Also, keep careful track of checks and debits so you don't bounce a check and get a bank charge, which is currently about $27 average per transaction.

KEEP MORE MONEY IN YOUR ACCOUNT
BY THE WAY YOU PAY BILLS

If you can pay your bills later without a penalty, you will have more money on hand in your account for other needs. One way to do this is to be aware that some bills list a due date that is not really the drop-dead past-due date. For example, we have found cable companies often ask for payment earlier than necessary and local property tax bills often come out in August or September but are not really due until the last day in December. For example, a cable bill that had a due date of the fifteenth of the month read, "Balance subject to a late charge of $4 if not paid within 35 days of due date." This means that this bill could have been paid as much as a month later. Look at all your bills, especially those you get intermittently such as insurance, to determine the true due date, after which your payment will be past due and there will be a penalty. Rick is now paying his $554 health insurance bill thirty days later than the due date listed on the bill because it turned out that the actual drop-dead due date was thirty days later than indicated. He had to read the fine print on the back of the bill to discover this fact. By paying this and other bills later, he has increased his cash flow.

Another bill-paying trick that can help your cash flow is to use an online bill-paying website, which most large companies provide these days. Just schedule payments so that they hit your account on the exact due date. This can save you the five business days you're supposed to plan for when your check is in the mail and you're not sure when the check is going to clear your bank. Another trick: If you get paid on the thirtieth of each month but have a major bill that is due on the twenty-eighth, you can often call that company and get them to move up their due date. A number of folks we know were able to do this with more than one major credit card company; one of them charged a bit more interest for moving the date up a week, but the other charged nothing.

On the credit side, set up direct deposit for any income you receive. Your money gets into your account faster, and it saves you a trip downtown. And it can come in handy if you have a debit and a credit racing for the bank at the same time. A prime example of this is Social Security. When you arrange for automatic deposit, the Social Security check will clear right after midnight on the day marked on the check. Since Social Security checks are never dispensed on weekends or legal holidays, you can benefit. For example, one of Tom's friends normally receives checks on the third of each month, but they will be deposited one or two days earlier if the third falls on a weekend.

Also, if you receive a number of checks each month, open a checking account that credits your account on the day that you make the deposit. Many business checking accounts do this, for example. Banks may charge a bit extra for business accounts, but if you keep a minimum balance there is often no charge.

KEEP MORE OF YOUR MONEY: CHANGE YOUR TAX WITHHOLDING

If you get a tax refund each year, that means you're giving the government your money to use for nothing. You should change your withholding so that you get a portion of that money each time you get paid and so can put that extra money in a bank. *Reader's Digest* reported that the average refund was $2,324, or $194 a month plus interest.

Summary: Money-Saving Tips for Banking Costs

- You can keep your money safe if it's in a bank insured by FDIC.
- Avoid check-balancing mistakes.
- Shop around for a bank with lower fees.
- Buy cheaper checks.
- Pay bills at last minute.
- Change amount of tax withholding.

Chapter 3

CABLE TELEVISION

⊞

*W*arm and fuzzy images do not come to mind when we think of cable companies. The problem with cable companies is that they have managed to become the only game in town. According to the Federal Communications Commission, cable rates went up 93 percent from 1996 to 2005. In 2003, according to a Consumers Union report on cable TV pricing and practices, typical prices increased 7 percent while inflation was only 1 percent. Following are some tips to take the bite out your cable bill.

IF COST GOES UP, THREATEN TO SWITCH

- *A call to the cable company can save you $20 a month for the same service.*

While satellite TV poses only a minor alternative to the virtual monopoly of cable, when cable rates jump again—and they will—the threat of switching to satellite might help lower your cable bill. While you probably don't want to go through the hassle of switching, which also locks you into a long-term contract, you could say that you are seriously considering it.

Rick did just that: He waved the satellite sword, as it were. When he received a huge increase in his monthly cable bill, he called the company and threatened to switch to satellite. Within a few minutes he was put in touch with a sweet-talking cable supervisor who offered him a "special deal" for a limited time. Rick did not fully understand the executive's explanation, but he did understand the money to be saved. His charges dropped from $70 a month to $50. The deal was only good for about a year and a half, but even so, the savings were over $300, and who knows, Rick could call again and maybe get a similar or the same offer. In other words, do call when the price goes up, and explain that you will be gone.

SUBSCRIBE TO NETFLIX AND LOWER YOUR CABLE COSTS

How often have you heard it? You have this great cable TV or satellite system with one hundred channels. But there's nothing on. How can that be? Simple: Many channels show the same programs. We have seen the same biography, such as the life story of General Patton for example, on A&E, the History Channel, the Military Channel, and the Biography Channel. These stations replay the same programs ad nauseam. Cinemax or some other pay channel? You still can't escape seeing the same program over and over because pay channels repeat things all the time. Example: *Sixteen Candles,* which came out in 1984 and seemingly has been on 1,984 times. Indeed, by the time this flick is about to finally disappear, Molly Ringwald, the star of the movie, will be sitting on a couch and pointing to the screen with her cane and saying, "See how pretty I was as a young girl?" Another problem with cable or satellite TV movies is the way they're cut. When you do find a movie you haven't seen, you will often see a notice before the film runs that says "edited for content" and "formatted to fit your screen" and "edited to run in the time allotted," meaning that what you are seeing is a butchered version of the actual movie—not to mention that it will be broken up by an army of ads. And to add insult to injury, the phrase "to run in the time allotted" means that the movie was cut so that the channel could show more advertisements. What's more, some of the people doing the cutting have the emotional sensitivity of a bull in a china shop, such as cutting a movie right in the middle of stirring scene. "Frankly, Scarlett," says Rhett Butler at the end of *Gone with the Wind*, "I don't—" Then, instead of "—give a damn," an ad for Viagra appears.

So you have to ask yourself a crucial question: What are you paying for? A friend of ours claims that most people, men and women, spend at least half an hour a day flipping through the channels, never really settling down to watch a particular program. And we have to agree.

But the big question is: Is there anything you can do? Is cable really worth the $70 or so dollars a month just to waste half an hour a day channel surfing? Imagine a system where you got perfectly clear reception of movies and programs you wanted to watch on demand with no ads and no "editing for content." This system is so good, it never experiences the all-too-common cable glitches no matter what the weather, and you get all of this for about $17 a month. Too good to be true? Well, not really. We're talking about Netflix, which we think is the best alternative to cable or satellite. And don't think of Netflix as being limited to only movies. You can find a variety of documentaries, past TV programs, and educational videos—plus the company keeps adding more DVDs to its lineup.

Using Netflix, you can get your cable service knocked down to the most basic plan, so that you get the local channels but not much else. In our area that service costs $7.35 a month.

Netflix is a well-run company with 8 million subscribers and warehouses all across the country. Start with the intro plan for about $17 dollars a month. This will give you access to over one hundred thousand movie titles to chose. They come in DVD form, and are usually mailed to you within twenty-

Netflix, a great way to save money on movies, and easy to do via mail.

four hours. Or use Netflix's streaming video capability to view titles instantly. And using the service is not a hassle. Netflix has designed a very simple return envelope that takes about ten seconds to use if you are clumsy—five seconds if you're not. The only problem with Netflix is that you will have an embarrassment of riches to choose from—and it will take time! We recommend that you go to the Netflix site for all the details, but suffice it to say, once you get set up, you could watch about one new movie a day with never a late fee and you can keep a movie as long as you like. And mailing not only is convenient but also saves you gas and a trip to a video store. If you implement this idea, you might pay $10 for minimal cable and $17 for Netflix for a total cost of $27 a month instead of $60 a month—a savings of $396 a year.

WAIT BEFORE YOU SUBSCRIBE TO HDTV

- *HDTV simply does not work properly in many areas.*

Ah, the promise of high-definition TV, which means clear, crisp, high-resolution digital pictures. It is a TV lover's dream. But there is a catch. In many areas it does not work. In fact, the digital channels are often worse, much worse than the analog channels.

This is because when analog is having problems, you might get snow or fuzz but you still get something. With digital you often get nothing, or the picture freezes or goes blank or you get big blocks of digital junk. Our investigation has revealed that while cable companies may offer this capability, their systems often cannot handle the increased load. There are many reasons for this, such as the cable companies trying to cram too many digital channels into bandwidth that is not large enough, sort of like cars not moving because on a highway because there are too many.

Bottom line: We think that HDTV is a great idea that will work very well at some point in the future. But in many areas it may be years before the systems can handle the demands of HDTV, so think twice before you rush out to buy an expensive flat-screen HDTV and sign up for HD cable service.

What we did—and why we decided against it for now— was to check with a neighbor or two who had already gotten the service from their cable service. When we did that in our area, we found out that it was not working well and that the cable company kept coming up with excuses but no fix.

Summary: Money-Saving Tips for Cable Television

- Threaten to drop service if cost goes up.
- Subscribe to Netflix.
- Wait before you subscribe to HDTV.

Chapter 4

CLOTHING

⊞

$\mathcal{C}$ lothing can be a major expense if you're not careful. Designer clothes and impulse buying, for example, can add a lot to your budget. But there are ways to slash your clothing costs while still looking stylish.

MAJOR COST-CUTTING CLOTHING STRATEGIES

BUY STORE-BRAND CLOTHING

- *Store-brand clothing is abundant, well made, and low cost.*

As we mentioned in our shopping section, store brands (also called private labels) are often very good deals. And store-brand clothing, in particular, is a shopper's paradise, not only for the low prices but for the quality, the variety, and the fantastic sale prices. In addition there is an astonishing range of clothing for virtually every style, age, and gender.

For example, Kmart has the Jaclyn Smith brand for fashion and the T.R. Bentley label for career women. In addition Kmart has the Route 66 casual clothing line, Beverly Hills Blues for young teens, Noah's Ark and Fox Hollow for young girls, and Sesame Street for children. JCPenney has the St. John's Bay, Worthington, and Arizona Jean Company store brands. But the story gets even better. Stores stand behind their brands, so you can return clothes for just about any reason.

But the real kicker is the price. Private labels are often marked up 80 percent while name brands are typically only marked up 50 percent—yet store-brand clothing will sell for much less than brand-name stuff. What this means is this: When store brands go on sale, they can be marked down substantially, in fact a lot more than brand-name clothing. And at the very end of a season, when stores put these garbs on close-out, you might get these clothes for half off or at even more of a discount.

HIGH FASHION FOR ROCK-BOTTOM PRICES

> • *Some store brands can be the height of fashion—*
> *if you know what to look for.*

Sharon Stone stunned Hollywood in 1996 when she arrived at the Oscars in a breathtaking turtleneck: "She was crowned the fashion queen of Hollywood for going against the grain, but infusing her own personal style to great effect," said an article on Yahoo's movies site. But the real secret took everyone by surprise. She had bought a mock turtleneck off the shelf from the Gap, which cost her about $20. So it's not how much you spend on clothes, it's how well they suit your unique body. Sharon Stone realized that her particular shape fit well with the way the Gap turtlenecks were cut. Every clothing manufacturer has its own way of cutting clothes for the average person, of a certain height and weight. Bottom line: Some manufactured clothing will fit you better than others, so look for a line of clothing that will make it look as if you had your clothes tailored.

Rick, for example, found that the cut of clothes at Lands' End fit his particular shape while some from the Gap did not, although Gap clothes certainly did fit Sharon Stone's stylish shape.

SHOP TILL YOU DROP AND BUY CHEAP CLOTHES THAT SUIT YOUR STYLE

You can save money and get stylish clothes no matter where you shop by starting with the closeout and discount bins. As we have pointed out elsewhere in this book, every store has these areas—even fancy stores or designer stores at the mall. People tend to buy what they look at first, so look at the cheap stuff first. If you don't find what you want, then move up to the next price level.

A teenager had this down to a science. She loved to shop but did not have a lot of money. She would spend a day going first to thrift stores, then to discount stores, and finally to the mall. At the end of the day she had bought something from just about every place she had visited and had even occasionally bought a designer item at full price, though only if it was just right for her look. And at the end of the day, she had spent less than $80 for several complete outfits plus accessories. Not too shabby.

BUY USED CLOTHING

There is a huge choice in used clothing. You can find it at yard sales, consignment shops, and thrift stores for as much as 90 percent off. In addition, once new clothes have been washed a number of times, they are indistinguishable from used.

MORE CLOTHING TIPS

SHOP "IRREGULARS" . . . MAYBE

As with other goods, clothing is available in irregulars—items that are damaged or abnormal in some way. Experts say that these are generally a good buy, but you have to be careful. "There are first, second, and third irregulars—third is the worst—and you can really get something bad," says one long-time retailer. For one thing, before you leave a store, make sure an item is perfect. One proprietor tells of receiving a famous-brand blouse with the left sleeve where the right should be and vice versa. And make sure you can take it back if the merchandise isn't something you want.

BUY IRREGULAR UNDERWEAR . . . MAYBE

As long as you stick to brand names like Hanes and Fruit of the Loom you will probably be okay. "On the other hand," one longtime retailer says, "when there are irregular sales on this particular item, you take a chance. Underwear is the one thing that gets the most wear of anything you put on your body. If you start out with a rip, flawed weave, or other problem, you can ruin it fast."

BUY ONLY GOOD SOCKS

"You're gambling if you buy irregulars," one retailer says.

WATCH TIE PURCHASES

Take care here. This is known in the trade as a "blind" item, probably because customers have no idea what they should cost—and you can pay through the neck, appropriately enough. A common practice is "keystoning," which means the store doubles the price it buys the tie for.

BUY BATHING SUITS ON SALE

If a woman can wait, bathing suits, at least in the North, go on sale about two weeks into July. Savings are great: 40 to 50 percent.

BUY DIRECT FROM THE MANUFACTURER

In some instances, it is possible to buy clothing direct from the manufacturer at a huge discount. For example, a person goes into a store such as Sears, finds a coat they like, and discovers who made the coat from the coat label. They then find a distributor in the yellow pages or on the Internet and ask for that coat at a 50 percent discount—and get it.

BUY YOUR BRIDAL GOWN FROM THE MANUFACTURER

Another direct sale route, one insider says, is bridal gown manufacturers. Every such manufacturer that this retail insider knows sells their merchandise wholesale. "Nine out of ten people who come into our store," he adds, "get the style, measurements, etc., and go right up to the manufacturer. They also get it at half price." Such direct dealings, our sources say, are possible on other items, especially large ones.

BUY YOUR FUR COAT FROM A FURRIER

A department store employee says that buying a fur coat in a department store is foolish. A furrier will cut one to exact size, give you a better selection and more attention, and charge a lot less (25 percent or more).

Summary: Money-Saving Tips for Clothing

- Buy store-brand clothing.
- Buy low-cost, high-fashion clothing in your style.
- Buy used clothing.
- Shop for "irregulars" . . . maybe.
- Don't buy irregular socks.

- Don't pay too much for a tie.
- Bathing suits go on sale in July.
- Buy expensive clothing directly from the manufacturer.
- Buy wedding gown from the manufacturer.
- Buy your fur coat from a furrier.

Chapter 5

CREDIT AND CREDIT CARDS

🛒

*A*s one insider said of the credit card business, "It's a license to steal." After they entice you with low-interest offers and then get you to charge a bunch of stuff, you find you're paying only the minimum each month. Then, out of the blue, your interest rate skyrockets to almost 30 percent. Calling the company does you no good—people at the "help" desk are not in the least sympathetic.

After a while you wonder if this was the company's plan all along, in other words, to get you in debt and then sock it to you with high rates that make it almost impossible to pay off your balance, not unlike a drug dealer who gets you hooked with free dope. And you would not be wrong in wondering that. But there are ways to cut your bills and even get help from your credit card company.

CUTTING CREDIT CARD RATES

HAGGLE FOR A LOWER CREDIT CARD INTEREST RATE

If you have a good record with a credit card company, chances are that you can slash your interest rate with a single call to the company. Just tell them that you've received other offers with lower annual percentage rates (APR) and were wondering if in lieu of your taking them, they can cut your rate. It's highly likely that they will. In 2002, as reported by *Consumer Reports*, the Massachusetts Public Interest Research Group had fifty customers, all with different credit backgrounds, call credit card companies and request a lower rate. Fifty-six percent of the time the companies agreed to do that, dropping the rates from an average 16 percent to 10.47 percent. So a majority of people got a lower rate just for asking. And even the long-distance call was toll free. It doesn't get much better than that these days.

WORK OUT A PAYBACK PROGRAM WITH THE CREDIT CARD COMPANY

- *Some credit card companies will put you on a payment plan with 6 percent interest.*

When a friend of ours became alarmed that his minimum monthly payment had gone up substantially, he called his credit card company, JPMorgan Chase. After a few questions he was routed to another office, where the person in charge offered to put him on the Balance Liquidation Program. This program would lower his interest rate to 6 percent from 29.99 percent and lower his monthly payment from $143 to $117 a month. They would close his revolving credit card account, which meant that he could pay off the balance in five years. He signed up for the program and the company was true to its word: The interest and payments dropped as promised.

Other banks have similar programs and one immediately wonders why they are so generous. Says Dan Sater, a finance specialist from Greenlawn, New York: "He was obviously a good customer and credit card companies want to hang on to people like that."

ELIMINATE LATE FEES

Here is a common complaint: You send your card payment five business days before the due date and yet it arrives late. So you are charged a late fee. In addition, this late fee goes onto your payment history. This in turn causes the interest rates on some of your other accounts to rise and, in turn, hurts your credit rating while at the same time making it harder to pay off your debts because of the increased interest.

You are not alone. Late charges for payments that were mailed in time have become such a problem that in May 2005 many people testified before the Senate Committee on Banking about these unfair practices. Yet Congress still does not seem ready to move even though it is aware of consumer discontent.

But all is not lost. There are a number of simple solutions. However, beware! Doing nothing is the worst thing you can do. So take charge and deal with it. Problem #1: You mailed your payment with time to spare but got charged anyway? Solution: Call the company and tell them the date you mailed your payment. Do this as soon as you notice a late charge on one of your bills. When this happens the first time, most companies will remove the charge. Also tell the business not to record a late payment on your credit history.

An even better idea is to consider paying online or by phone. These days many companies have phone and/or website payment services. Some charge for their phone bill-paying function—it will still likely be less than a late payment—but few charge for their online sites. We recommend that you use the online payment option whenever possible, as you can schedule your payment to be processed on the precise day that the bill is due—not a day earlier. This gives you maximum use of your cash. Phone payments are often credited on the day that you call with no choice as to the processing date.

When using online services read the fine print. Each one is different. For example, some accept payments up to closing time on the due date, while others will charge extra for crediting your account on the same day. Some will accept payments on Saturday, others won't. A few may charge for the service.

Make a Note of Your Agreement

*W*hen you get a credit card company to do what you want, don't stop there. Make a note of what you agreed to, whom you talked to, the office that person was in, the date and time, and anything else. This can be of considerable help if you find out later that what you agreed to is not taking place and you have to make a follow-up call. So, for example, if you need to get a late fee removed and not have your late payment show up on your credit history, make a full note of your conversation and then repeat what you wrote back to the person at the credit card office so that there is no mistake about what was agreed upon.

RE-AGING AN ACCOUNT: HOW TO REMOVE PAST-DUE AMOUNTS

- *Re-aging, starting your account over, can remove past-due notices and restore your credit rating.*

If you think you have ruined your credit rating, there might be a way to pull yourself back. While not a magic solution, re-aging—starting your account over—can go a long way toward repairing your credit *if* (and that's a big *if*) you stick to the terms of your agreement with the lender.

And it turns out that knowing the exact right term might save you hundreds or thousands of dollars. In this case, the magic word is *re-aging,* which means that your account, which might have been behind a payment or two, can get a fresh slate.

Here's an example from www.credit.com on its page about re-aging. "Let's say you are three months late on one of your credit cards. If you can convince the credit card provider to re-age your account, it's as if those three months never happened. You still owe the same amount of money, but the late fees stop and you are no longer considered delinquent. Your missed payments are simply ignored. Re-aging an account can be really good for your credit score. A big 'late' blemish comes off your account and it's considered current." Still, as we said, re-aging is not a perfect solution because you still have to come up with payments and meet all your due dates.

In addition, there are federal guidelines for re-aging. These include that borrowers should demonstrate that they have the means and the inclination to repay the loan, accounts need to be nine months old or more, re-aging cannot occur more than once every twelve months, and a lender cannot loan any new money until the existing loan amount is reduced past the point where the problem occurred.

If you do arrive at an agreement over the phone, take full notes on the terms that you agreed to. However, as with just about any transaction with a credit card company, also ask that the official at the company send you a copy of your agreement in writing.

OTHER CREDIT TIPS

TO RESOLVE A DISPUTE WITH A MERCHANT, CONTACT YOUR CREDIT CARD COMPANY

- *Use your credit card company to help with a billing problem.*

If you have a dispute with a charge on your account, or you're not happy with a product or service, contact the company that made the charge and try to resolve the problem. If it is not cooperative, and you have documentation to back up your claim, call your credit card company for help.

For example, Rick found that a monthly charge started to appear on his card statement after he signed up for a "free" trial period on a website. Talking with customer service at the Internet company did no good. They agreed to stop any future charges but would not refund past charges even though he had not used the website after the initial free trial period. Undaunted, he enlisted the help of his credit card company. A quick call from the card company to the Internet service quickly resolved the problem and the past charges were refunded. Why? As the credit card employee explained, the Internet company could have been "black-balled by the credit card company, making it very difficult for it to continue business on the Internet."

Is the Internet Safe?

*W*hile some people are wary of using websites for financial transactions, they are quite safe. Just make sure that your Web address (the URL in the browser window) starts with *https*—that is, an extra s (for *secure*) after the normal *http*.

This means that you are on a secure page and that you should have no problem with your transaction.

PAY CASH IF YOU CAN

Studies have shown that people spend more with a credit card, about 15 to 20 percent more. After all, it's only plastic and you don't have to come up with the actual cash for at least a month or maybe for years. So if you really are trying to get a handle on your finances, leave those cards in a drawer and leave temptation behind. Instead take along a set amount of cash that you have to live with. We know that it's un-American but it will keep you from getting further in debt.

UPPING YOUR CREDIT SCORE

Credit scores were established in 1989 by the Fair Isaac Corporation, commonly called FICO, to give employers a quick way to establish one's degree of creditworthiness. To get better interest rates, indeed to get credit, it is important to keep an eye on your credit score; it can mean literally thousands of dollars lost or saved. Following are some tips from credit expert Dan Sater to manage your score so it's accurate and as high as possible.

First, get your credit reports from the three major credit bureaus, Experian, TransUnion, and Equifax, by going to www.annualcreditreport.com. The government allows you to get one report free per year, but you should also get the scores because these are what prospective lenders go by. Check the items on all the reports. If you see any mistakes, write the company and point these out. If your identification is in question you can send proof of this.

The credit company has thirty days to answer your complaint, during which time they theoretically will check with your listed debtor to see if the information is accurate. Many times, however, the debtor won't respond within the thirty days and the credit company will be required to remove the items you challenge. Note that there are errors all the time.

Once you have the score corrected, you can do a number of things to continue to improve it.

As we mentioned before, sign up for automatic bill payment. You want to be sure you're on time, because credit card companies will hit you with penalties and fees when you're not.

If you're applying for a loan, keep spending down and try to pay off some of your debt. Double-check that credit limits are posted. Some retailers and others don't do this, which leads FICO to assume that the cards are maximized, and this can result in as much as a fifty-point drop in your score.

Don't apply for a lot of credit cards. This will trigger a review by the lender and can reduce your score. However, if you're trying to get a mortgage you can apply for many credit cards without the activity having a negative effect on your credit. If you have too many credit cards, don't close them out with the idea that your score will get a bounce. Actually, when you do that the percentage of credit you're tapping into will go up, a bad indicator. The more credit options you have to tap into, the better your credit picture looks. Also, closing out cards will lower the average account age, which is another no-no because account age is an important factor in determining the score.

GET THE BEST LOAN YOU CAN

Some people who have lousy credit assume that they won't be able to get a loan, but that's not always true. In fact, we have found that most individual stores will gladly lend you the money when you buy a product there. So the appliance store will usually be delighted to finance your new refrigerator and that office supply store will set up an account so that you can buy a new laser printer. While the interest on this type of loan will be substantial, it is better than no loan if you are really in need of something essential like a refrigerator.

Need an Extra $100? It May Be There for the Taking

*A*ccording to Coinstar, the leader in self-service coin count-ing, the average household has about $99 in loose change just sitting around. The problem is that it's often a few quarters here and a couple of dimes there. But if you spend a few min-utes gathering all those coins hidden in your couch, your car, your pocket or purse, and your drawers, you might be pleas-antly surprised at how much money you have on hand.

Summary: Money-Saving Tips for Credit Costs

- Haggle for a lower interest rate.
- Work out a payback program with credit card company.
- Resolve disputes through credit card company.
- Save by the way you pay your bills.
- Pay cash if you can.
- Eliminate late fees.
- Re-age an account.
- Up your credit score.
- Get the best score you can.
- Get a loan even when you're tapped out.

Chapter 6

DRUGS AND PRESCRIPTIONS

🛒

*A*ccording to a congressional report, "The United States has the highest drug prices in the world." As a result many seniors have to choose between buying the drugs they need and paying for their groceries, a cruel fact that was revealed in a survey by the Harvard School of Public Health. Indeed, many Americans have resorted to technically breaking the law by, according to a report by CNN, buying their drugs in Canada in an attempt to save money.

What is wrong with this picture? Is it right or fair that people who need medicine but have a limited income suffer? Is there something that they or anyone else who is saddled with high prescription prices can do? As one senior put it, "The answer, fortunately, is a resounding yes," and in the pages that follow we will show you exactly how to dramatically cut—or perhaps *slash* is a better word—your drug costs.

PRESCRIPTIONS
USE GENERIC DRUGS

- *Authorities say you can save up to 80 percent, with generic drugs that are the same quality as brand-name drugs.*

When most people think of "generic" products, they picture low-cost, bottom-of-the-barrel products. Therefore they assume that generic drugs will be of a lower quality than brand-name drugs. But in most cases nothing could be further from the truth.

The word *generic* has a very different meaning when it comes to prescription drugs. Generics are drugs that are no longer protected by a company's patent. After the patent for an expensive name-brand drug runs out, companies that manufacture generic drugs may be able to make the drug at a much lower cost. Yet this does not affect its quality. According to the Food and Drug Administration (FDA), "Generic drugs are identical to their brand-name counterparts in dosage form, safety, strength, route of administration, quality, performance, and intended use. Generics also go through a rigorous scientific review to ensure both safety and effectiveness."

So, now you know that you have nothing to fear with generics. Just how much could you save? It couldn't be that much, could it? Wrong. The National Association of Chain Drug Stores stated in 2004 that "the average price of a generic prescription drug was $28.74, while the average price of a brand-name prescription drug was $96.01." The FDA stated that "generic drugs cost about 30 percent to 80 percent less than brand name drugs."

But you might be thinking there can't be that many generic drugs. People probably don't have any choice but to pay the higher brand-name price because a particular drug is not yet a generic. And again, you would be wrong. The FDA reported, "As of June 2005, there were 11,167 drugs listed in the FDA's Orange Book, and about 8,400 had generic counterparts." In other words, more than 75 percent of the drugs could be bought as generics.

So we hope you get the message. To save money on prescriptions, always ask your doctor if a generic would be as effective, and always buy generics when they are effective and available, period.

But this is just the start in terms of how you can save on prescriptions. When you put all of the following tips together, your savings could be astounding. But there is a catch. (Aha, you think. I knew there was a catch.) The catch is this: You'll need to know a bit of the lingo of drugs and prescriptions and will have to involve your doctor so that he or she understands not just your physical but also your financial needs. And always be aware that children are particularly sensitive consumers of medications and may respond differently from adults to the substitution of a generic for a brand name. Where children are concerned, your pediatrician is your best source of information.

MAKE SURE YOUR PRESCRIPTION ALLOWS GENERICS

Prescription forms vary from state to state, and so we recommend that people take some time to become familiar with forms and the doctor's indecipherable scratching so that they don't get stuck.

For example, Chicago waitress Joan Mitchell went to the pharmacy to buy a drug she needed to keep her blood pressure in check. Her doctor had prescribed Prinivil, a name-brand product, and without asking her, had checked the box on the prescription form that prevented the druggist from substituting a generic. Thus Joan was left with no choice but to pay for the much-higher-priced drug. Yet in Joan's case the generic medication lisinopril was available, which would have saved her over 48 percent.

Generic Medication Information
☐ Yes, I authorize DrugSource to dispense generic medications.
☐ No, I do not authorize DrugSource to dispense generic medications and understand that refusal of generic medication may impact my co-payment.

A typical checkbox in which a physician specifies that a generic drug can be dispensed.

Six months later, at her next doctor visit, Joan asked the doctor to issue another prescription, only this time she specifically asked that he check the box to allow a generic substitution. The lesson Joan learned applies to everyone who gets a prescription. Every patient should make sure that they can buy a generic if they so choose. While many people are hesitant to question their doctors, they must get their doctors to work with them so that they can control their health costs.

An Astonishing Failure/Success Story

*A*t least one drug trial was funny—very funny. A certain blue pill was passed out to men in England to see if it would have a beneficial effect on their cardiovascular conditions. It didn't work, so Pfizer asked for all the unused pills in the study to be returned. Pfizer ran into resistance. Small wonder. The pill had another positive effect—and still does. Its name is Viagra.

IF A GENERIC ISN'T AVAILABLE, USE A COMPARABLE BUT DIFFERENT GENERIC

- *Even when a generic is not available, you may not have to pay a high price.*

What if your doctor prescribes a drug that is not available as a generic and that costs a lot of money? Are you stuck with paying that high price? The answer is probably not. The FDA tells us, "Even when a particular branded drug has no generic, a very similar member of the same drug class may be available.

For this reason, instead of asking doctors whether a particular brand-name drug has a generic version, patients should ask whether there is a generic available that can be used to treat their problem."

Since there were more than 11,167 drugs listed in the FDA's Orange Book in 2005, it is unlikely that your doctor will be familiar with all the possible choices for your condition. In addition, many doctors are unaware of the costs of specific drugs, according to the FDA.

Perhaps you can help your doctor find a good generic substitute. For example, your pharmacist has a wealth of information, much more than what the average doctor knows about drugs. The pharmacist deals with prescriptions every day of the week. So in addition to speaking with your doctor, speak to your pharmacist.

A Winning Recipe

When Tom found out that a relative was taking a blood pressure medication called Lotrel—the prescription was Lotrel 5/20—which cost more than $200 for a ninety-day supply, he asked his pharmacist if there was any generic substitute. There wasn't, but the pharmacist was able to suggest an alternative: If the doctor approved and would be willing to prescribe two generic medications, one a 20-mg tablet and the other a 5-mg tablet, the pharmacist believed they would have the same effect as the originally prescribed dose of Lotrel. The doctor agreed, and Tom's relative was able to fill the new prescriptions at a cost of only $25 for a ninety-day supply of both medications, a savings of more than $175 per refill, or more than $700 a year.

If there's no suitable generic on the market, don't despair. There may be a new generic that's arriving soon. After a drug has been on the market about twenty years, its patent runs out and its generic version may become available. For example, the patent for the well-known drug Lipitor will expire soon, so a generic should be available in the near future.

The FDA Orange Book lists patent expiration dates for prescription medicine, and a generic may be available after those dates. In the online version you can look up brand-name drugs you are taking and find out when the patent will expire: Visit http://www.fda.gov/cder/orange/.

Also, to find a list of drugs on the Internet that will be coming off patent, do a Web search for "prescriptions patents expiration." This should bring up a number of sites that list patent expirations. (Unfortunately, there is no website that consistently lists upcoming expirations.)

AVOID TAKING DTC DRUGS

- *Drugs that are advertised on TV are often very expensive and not the best choice.*

Be aware of "DTC" or direct-to-consumer marketing. It is a relatively new tool in the bag of tricks that greed-crazed drug manufacturers use to get you to buy the latest expensive prescription medicine and also to convince a number of people that they have a serious condition that they should deal with. Drug companies spent $4.8 billion in advertising in 2006. During that same period roughly one-third of patients asked their doctors about an advertised medicine and the doctors gave patients the drug they requested 44 percent of the time, according to a study by Harvard School of Public Health. Yet this kind of advertising is illegal in most of the world, including Europe. These ads are designed to create an emotional and not a medical response. (See the sidebar "Ben Casey Redux.")

When you see an ad for a new drug and want to rush out to try it, take a deep breath and reconsider. People who use a new drug in the first year are basically guinea pigs. New drugs have not been tested on large populations. When drug use moves from thousands of patients to millions, unforeseen side effects often come to light. (See the sidebar "A Really Bad Side Effect.") A prime example is the infamous case of the expensive name-brand prescription drug Vioxx (which has been taken off the market). It was sold to treat osteoarthritis and acute pain. The commonly available drugs ibuprofen and naproxen, however, were also used to treat these same conditions—and these cheap over-the-counter drugs often worked just as well or better for many patients than Vioxx. And these plain-Jane drugs, it turned out, were much safer. After five years of widespread use, it was found that Vioxx led to an increased risk of heart attacks and strokes. (We wonder how that bald-headed guy gamboling along a beach with his dog in the TV ad made out.) As a result, it was withdrawn from sale. Before removing the drug in 2004, Merck, the maker of Vioxx, had made as much as $2.5 billion a year selling Vioxx, according to the Reuters news service.

Some ads are for conditions that may not need to be treated. The advertisement for urinary drugs that allows men to use the bathroom less frequently is also an appeal to manliness and to help men avoid embarrassment. We recommend that in general you tune out these ads unless you are pretty sure you have a medical condition that these prescriptions might help treat. Then you should ask your doctor for a full examination and discuss all types of treatment, including low-cost ones. Note also that pharmaceutical companies will advertise and tout a new drug as a remarkable advance in medicine that everyone who might benefit should try. Yet before you rush out and pop some of these pills, read this joke that doctors tell among themselves: "Wait a year before prescribing a new drug to your patients; wait five years before prescribing the same drug to anyone in your family."

A Really Bad Side Effect

*I*ncidentally, we always get a kick out of manufacturers ticking off possible side effects of a new drug. We remember one that was available to treat fungus in toenails, and the side effects seemingly included every terrifying medical problem that humanity has ever endured, including death. Anyone who took that drug would need another—to treat their insanity. We can see the funeral director approaching the deceased spouse. "Oh," the director would say, "your husband has the most beautiful toenails I've ever seen."

CONSULT WITH YOUR DOCTOR

Always consult with your doctor before taking any medicine, and this even includes over-the-counter drugs. However, if your doctor is uncooperative, we also recommend that you find a new doctor.

TALK TO YOUR PHARMACIST

- *Your pharmacist may have the best understanding and overview of the drugs you take.*

Perhaps one of the best-kept secrets in health care is that your pharmacist will usually talk to you for free when you pick up your prescription. Phil Alexander, the chief pharmacist at

Kmart in Morehead City, North Carolina, told Rick, "The pharmacist is a very valuable resource who may even have a more complete picture than your doctor of the medicines you are taking." Phil added that you should "find a pharmacy where the druggist will spend time explaining your medication to you. You should even be able to call him or her on the phone if need be."

Phil suggests having your pharmacist periodically review your total drug regimen. By doing this he or she can spot possible drug interactions as well as drugs that may duplicate each other and cause overmedication. What do you do if your pharmacist doesn't have the time to talk to you? Phil said, "If he or she doesn't have the time, then go somewhere else."

Will Your Pharmacist Really Spend Time with You?

Kmart pharmacy gives you this handout when you buy a prescription: "Your KMART Pharmacist is always available to answer questions about your prescription."

PRESCRIPTION DISCOUNTS

GET FREE DRUGS

- *Doctors will give you free samples.*

If you are stuck with taking an expensive name-brand prescription drug, ask your doctor for free samples. Pharmaceutical companies give doctors tons of free samples to get patients to try their drugs, so you can benefit. Indeed, Tom's wife had to take a very expensive drug named Arimidex— more than $350.89 for a month's supply. Her doctor supplied her with free samples from June to November, or around $1,755 worth of medication.

BUY PILLS IN DOUBLE DOSES, THEN CUT THEM IN HALF

One of the best ways to save a lot of money on drugs is to buy a double dose and then cut the pills in half. While this works with many pills, it does not work with all (especially capsules and timed-release pills). Ask your doctor or pharmacist. You can buy a small cutting device called a "pill splitter" that will quickly and accurately slice a tablet. The savings are often quite dramatic, typically as much as 40 percent. We have even seen cases where a bottle of large-dose pills costs less than a bottle with smaller-dose pills, half the size. (Go figure!)

But is cutting pills in half safe? Apparently it is, assuming the tablet is scored and can be split cleanly and evenly. One of the largest health insurers in Arizona, UnitedHealthcare, urged members to do just that to save money. UnitedHealthcare even gave pill splitters to its policyholders and charged half-price copayments for patients who split their pills in half.

To use a pill cutter, just place pill in cutter . . .

*. . . snap cutter
top down . . .*

*. . . and pill is
neatly sliced—
and so is the
money you'll
spend on some
drugs.*

BUY PILLS IN UNOPENED BOTTLES

Buying a full, unopened bottle of medicine that you know you need and will use can save you a substantial amount of money. The pharmacist will save time not having to count out the pills and put them in their own container. In addition, the record keeping for a full bottle is much simpler for the pharmacy and you will be buying in bulk—so expect bulk savings.

COMPARISON SHOP PRESCRIPTIONS AT DIFFERENT STORES

Don't buy all your drugs from the same pharmacy. You can comparison shop for drugs—buying them wherever they're cheapest. You can shop over the phone but make sure that you compare apples to apples. When you make the call, ask for a price on the same number of pills, dosage, and brand. However, there is one downside to shopping around: You need to be aware of all the pills you are taking and periodically ask your pharmacist to review your medications (see elsewhere in this section). When you do, you will need to tell him or her about other drugs you are taking, that is, drugs that you buy from other pharmacies.

DON'T ASSUME A DISCOUNT IS NOT AVAILABLE
- *Always ask how to qualify for a discount.*

Never assume that you have to pay the asking price for drugs even if you must pay for them out of pocket. Even an insurance plan with a high deductible or one that doesn't pay for prescriptions may entitle you to a discount. Many pharmacies offer discounts to seniors and parents of young children. Always ask your pharmacy if you qualify and if it participates in your insurer's plan. If it does not, you might want to shop around to find a pharmacy that does. Don't be shy—always ask.

BUY LOW-COST GENERIC DRUGS AT WAL-MART, TARGET, ETC.

For a while now, Wal-Mart has been offering hundreds of generic prescription drugs at $4 for a thirty-day supply and $10 for a ninety-day supply. Recently the retailer expanded the same deal to one thousand different over-the-counter (OTC) drugs. The prices may have gone up by the time you read this, but it's Wal-Mart and cheap prices are its stock-in-trade. Other companies, such as Target, which is Wal-Mart's top competitor, and Walgreens, also offer cheap generics. To view the fantastic array of cheap drugs that Wal-Mart offers, go to www.walmart.com/pharmacy.

DO YOU NEED THE DRUG?

Before you decide to get a drug, you should ask a fundamental question, one that most people don't ask: Are you sick enough to need drugs? Many doctors say that the only reason they prescribe drugs is because patients want them to. A doctor with the American Pharmaceutical Association advises people "to give this some serious thought. Decide if you're really sick enough." The same thing applies to OTC drugs. Are you sick enough to use them? If you're not, don't waste your money taking something.

Ben Casey Redux

Years ago, there was a popular television program called *Ben Casey*, about a tough doctor practicing in a Los Angeles hospital. The day after each show aired, and no matter how off-the-wall the disease of the week was, doctors were inundated with calls from concerned patients.

USE THE CHEAPEST DRUG THAT WORKS FOR YOU

If you have a condition that requires a drug, it is good to remember that the effectiveness of drugs is often an individual thing. Some drugs work well with some people and not well with others. And in many cases—and here's the money-saving tip—a lower-priced drug may actually work better than a higher-priced one. "I was on one brand of beta blocker for high blood pressure," says Gene Dowling, a freelance writer in Los Angeles, and "I asked my doctor if I could try anything cheaper because it was costing me about $70 a month. I got another brand that was just as good—even better—and it cost me around $50 less a month. I saved $600 a year."

A good rule of thumb is to start with an inexpensive, commonly available drug for your condition and see if it helps. If it doesn't, then try a pricier drug and then move on up the price ladder until you find a drug that works. There is a further advantage to starting with well-known low-cost drugs. These have often been used for decades by millions of people and therefore their side effects are well-known, too.

NONPRESCRIPTION DRUGS

USE OVER-THE-COUNTER DRUGS INSTEAD OF PRESCRIPTION DRUGS

Many OTC drugs that used to be available only by prescription are now on the shelves of your local pharmacy. In fact, in recent years more prescription drugs than ever are now easily and cheaply available as OTC medications. For example, Claritin became available without a prescription in 2002. Ibuprofen (such as Advil), naproxen (such as Aleve), and cetirizine (such as Zyrtec) all used to be available only by prescription but now can be bought over the counter. OTC drugs, of course, are usually much cheaper than prescription medicine.

So finding an OTC drug (consult with your pharmacist) that treats your conditions solves some costly problems. First, you save money; second, you don't have to get a prescription and incur a costly visit to a doctor; and third, you don't have to pay the extra cost of having a pharmacist fill your prescription (due to complex paperwork, there is an added overhead cost to filling each prescription in addition to the cost of the medicine itself). Of course, you should use common sense here. A child's fever or rash always requires at very least a call to a pediatrician; this is not the time to check with a pharmacist for an OTC remedy in order to save money on a doctor's visit or prescription.

You should also check with your doctor any time you are considering substituting an OTC for a medication that has already been prescribed for you. It is rarely a good idea to change course from a prescription medication to the OTC alternative when the treatment is already underway, and you should never do so without checking with a medical doctor, especially when the patient is a child.

SAVE 40 PERCENT ON STORE-BRAND ("PRIVATE-LABEL") OTC DRUGS

While buying OTC drugs will save you a lot of money, you can save even more because many OTC drugs are available as "private-label" products at bigger chain stores. For example, Wal-Mart sells the Equate brand for a variety of OTC drugs. The savings are considerable. When we compared eleven OTC products at Kmart, we found that the private-label products were 44 percent cheaper on average than the better-known national name-brand product.

So how much could you save with a rock-bottom-priced private-label OTC drug versus a brand-name prescription? Let's take the example of Vioxx. (We're sorry to keep picking on Vioxx, but it is a great example.) Prescription pills of Vioxx could cost as much as $3 apiece while the same dosage of brand-name Advil ibuprofen might cost 60 cents (a savings of 90 percent) and OTC ibuprofen might cost all of 36 cents. Do the math for a year (365 days): a person taking Vioxx might spend $1,095, the person taking Advil might spend $219, and a person taking the private-label ibuprofen might spend $131.

"Cut Rate" Strikes Again

*J*ose Rodriguez, an accountant in Hoboken, New Jersey, says that he's gotten great discounts on vitamin and mineral supplements. "I know they have a high markup—around 70%—so I've been able to negotiate the price down at least 50% many, many times. In fact, the manager of the Walgreens store where I deal nicknamed me 'Cut Rate.' Now I never even have to ask for a discount. The only question is how much I'm getting."

STORE DRUGS PROPERLY

No matter how much you save when buying drugs, all that can be lost if the drugs are stored in the wrong place and go bad. In general, moisture, heat, and light—from sun or fluorescent lights—are enemies of drugs. Many drugs, an American Pharmaceutical pharmacist points out, "are stored in the bathroom, where they are subject to a lot of heat and moisture." Another bad spot: the kitchen. Unless otherwise instructed, the best place for drugs is a cool, dark, dry place. A linen closet can be a good spot.

Summary: Money-Saving Tips for Drugs

- Make sure you need a drug.
- Avoid taking DTC drugs.

- Use generic drugs—they're cheap and good.
- Ask pharmacist for advice on getting cheap drugs.
- Use the cheapest drug that works for you.
- Use over-the-counter instead of prescription drugs.
- Use free samples from doctor.
- Buy pills in double doses, then cut them in half.
- Buy unopened bottles of medication.
- Buy prescriptions at different stores, whichever is cheapest.
- Don't assume a discount is not available. .
- Buy drugs at Wal-Mart, Target, etc.

Chapter 7

ENERGY BILLS

Home heating fuel is a major expense. And if the price of oil goes up in the future, the price of heating fuel will follow. In addition, wasting heat is like tossing dollars into a roaring fire. By making your home tighter and more heat efficient, you will feel more comfortable and save plenty. Here's what you can do.

LESS-KNOWN WAYS TO SAVE ON ENERGY COSTS

FILL UP YOUR HEATING FUEL TANK IN SUMMER

The owner of a propane business, Ray Teel, gave Rick this tip. "Fuel prices are very seasonal," he said. "If you fill up in the summer you can get a discount, as much as 30 percent less than what it will cost you in October."

SIGN UP FOR BUDGET BILLING

While the following tip will not lower your bill, it will make it much more manageable. "We would encourage people to sign up for budget billing, which helps smooth out the bills," said Jeff Tilghman of Yankee Gas Services Company in Connecticut. This means that you pay a regular amount for oil on a monthly basis—which makes it much easier to budget. Generally these plans run for twelve months and are based on the projected cost of oil for your home. If the cost exceeds your budgeted amount at the end of the twelve months, you may find that you still owe the oil company some more money. If it's less, you may be owed a refund.

Put Your Utility and Heating Expenses on a Budget

A budget plan may be available from your electric utility company or propane dealer in addition to your heating oil company. Ask.

REPLACE, REPAIR, CLEAN YOUR FURNACE

Getting your furnace to work at top efficiency will pay for itself very quickly. Sal Camera, manager of Alpine Heating & Cooling Company in East Haven, Connecticut, said, "It's the best investment you can make. You can cut 30 percent to 40 percent off your heating bills." The national average home heating bill is projected to be about $2,600 for 2008–2009 (and much more in very cold areas). This means that spending as much as $1,000 (or about 40 percent of the projected home heating bill) could pay for itself in the first year. A good rule of thumb is to replace your furnace if it is more than fifteen years old.

NOTE: Even if your furnace is in good shape, give it an annual checkup. Replacing furnace filters, keeping your furnace clean, and sealing any leaks in heating ducts can all make a considerable difference in the amount you pay for home heating fuel. Also remember to replace furnace filters every month or so as needed during the heating season.

GET TOU RATES

TOU, or "time-of-use," rates are one of the best-kept secrets of electric companies when it comes to saving money on electric bills. A survey by the American Energy Institute revealed that about half of investor-owned utilities offered TOU rates to customers in an attempt to balance power load demands and to give peak-time electric use some relief. However, only 1 percent of customers took advantage of TOU because, our guess is, they simply didn't know anything about it.

We know TOU can save you hundreds of dollars a year because we have it from Rick himself. Last year, Rick says, "I saved over $600 using my utility's time-of-use program and I have saved around $6,000 over the ten years since I've been using it." How does he know exactly how much he has saved? "Because my utility company, Progress Energy, prints what I save on my bill." All TOU requires is that the customer have heavy-use electric appliances and perhaps change heating and cooling thermostat settings during peak hours. To get his great savings, all Rick has to do is run the electric clothes dryer during off-peak hours.

Most TOU programs have two schedules, one for the warm weather and one for the cold. Off-peak typically starts at 9 PM and runs to 6 AM or 9 AM depending on the time of year. Weekends are all off-peak, as are all holidays. If you are interested, call your power company and ask to speak with the official who is in charge of TOU. That employee can then read your electric bill, ask a few questions, and within minutes tell you how much you could save each month. To enroll in the TOU plan, a utility will install a special meter, usually at no cost. This meter keeps track of the times when power has been used.

The fiscal benefits of TOU are not restricted to home use. Businesses can also take advantage. A deejay at a small radio

Billing
Residential-
Time of Use
Demand rate

195 OLD NASSAU RD - 30 Days			
Basic customer charge			9.85
On-peak KWH	496 kwh x	$0.05902	29.2739
Off-peak KWH	908 kwh x	$0.04528	41.1142
On-peak KW	4.13 kw x	$5.02000	20.7326
3% North Carolina sales tax			3.03
Total due			$104.00

Current month Time-of-Use Savings for meter RB7504: $ 41.66, as compared with rate RES

Current twelve month Time-of-Use Savings for meter RB7504: $ 608.42

Statement showing Rick's savings of more than $600 yearly under the
TOU program of his local power company.

station told Rick that the station had saved $4,800 a year simply by switching to TOU. "All we did was change the meter," the deejay said. "We didn't do anything different from what we had been doing before." A golf course in North Carolina saved more than $10,000 a year by charging up its golf carts during off-peak hours.

LOWER THE THERMOSTAT

How many people heat their entire home when they spend most of the evening in one room watching TV? Many home heating systems are set up to keep the entire house at one temperature and are not capable of "spot heating"—that is, heating only one room while the others are colder. However, with a little ingenuity, you can do just that.

Get an efficient space heater or an electric throw blanket for the TV or den. That way you can turn down the heat and still be very comfortable in your favorite room for the evening. Also, turn the thermostat down to 55 degrees when you are not home, and an hour before you go to bed, since the house will stay relatively warm for that time period. Turning the house temperature down to 62 degrees and keeping only one room warm can save an average of about $200 during the winter, according to *Good Housekeeping*. In another example, turning your thermostat down a single degree Fahrenheit can save you 25 to 30 gallons of fuel a year or around $100 in the northeast climate (based on estimated 2008–2009 fuel costs), according to the Maine Public Utilities Commission.

TURN DOWN YOUR WATER HEATER

Check that your hot water heater is set to 120 degrees and not 140 degrees (the normal setting when the heater comes from the factory). This will save you a considerable amount of money over time—perhaps $30 a year—and help your heater last longer.

GET A FREE ENERGY AUDIT

It may seem like a case of the fox guarding the henhouse, but your electric utility or your gas utility may offer free home energy audits. These audits by professionals can pinpoint ways that your home is wasting energy. We suggest that if you get such an audit, you should not feel compelled to do everything that the auditors suggest, but rather focus on those steps that will cost the least and be the easiest to do—at least in the beginning. The public utility of Rocky Mount, North Carolina, which offers such a program, states, "An audit of your home or business may significantly reduce your utility expenses." In addition, there are a number of do-it-yourself energy audits that have been put together by government agencies, such as the U.S. Department of Energy's "Do-It-Yourself Home Energy Audits" at their website: http://www.eere.energy.gov/consumer/your_home.

GET HELP FROM YOUR UTILITY
   • *Get your power company to pay you or loan you money.*

It may be surprising, but your utility company may not be the devil (at least not always). It may even be your friend. Utilities can offer a number of ways to help you save money and reduce your use of power. There are often a variety of programs, including low-interest loans, that will allow you to make your home more energy efficient, and discounts for energy-efficient homes. In addition there are "load management programs." If you participate in these, the electric company will pay you money (not a typo—go back and reread). For example, the public utility of Rocky Mount, North Carolina, can attach devices to your hot water heater, air conditioner, or heating strip. If electric demand exceeds peak capacity the power company will, by radio control, turn these devices off temporarily. This utility states, "Customers participating in any of the load management programs usually do not notice when their load management switch is activated." In turn the company will pay you between $2 and $15 a month for the privilege. Service is guaranteed by this utility, which will remove the devices at no cost if you don't like the program.

Would You Pay $9.50 to Save Almost $300?

*W*al-Mart is now selling its own brand of Energy Star—compliant fluorescent lightbulbs that are the equivalent of 60-watt incandescent lightbulbs. (You will learn more about Energy Star later in this chapter.) A package of six bulbs sells for about $9.50, and it's claimed that each bulb will save $47 over its life. Multiply that by six and you have about $300.

TIGHTEN UP YOUR HOME

In order to be complete, we have added the following standard tips for tightening up your home, but we have also added some little-known information about each tip. The best advice is to do the easiest things first and then tackle the more difficult things. Making your home energy efficient can cut your heating and cooling expenses by 30 percent or more, add value to your home, and make you more comfortable. Take advantage of situations as they arise. For example, if you need to replace some windows, make sure that you replace them with the most energy-efficient ones. If you do some home remodeling and tear open an outside wall, add insulation to that wall—it will add very little cost to your home improvement and help conserve energy.

INSTALL STORM WINDOWS AND STORM DOORS TO CUT HEATING COSTS

Lots of heat can be lost through ordinary window glass, making your furnace work harder and use more fuel. Storm windows and doors help prevent this. They provide dead air space between themselves and regular glass and can cut heat loss in half.

INSTALL HOMEMADE STORM WINDOWS

If you don't have the money for regular glass storm windows, you can make plastic ones that are just as good for keeping cold out and heat in. You can do it a couple of ways. One is to use masking tape to attach thin drop-cloth-gauge plastic (your hardware store dealer can tell you the thickness or gauge to use) to one side of a screen and then install the screen in the window. Alternatively, cut a sheet of plastic big enough to cover the window and then tape its edges to the molding. Cheap plastic storm window kits are also available. Another fuel saver: Close off the porch with plastic during the winter.

INSTALL INSULATION

Insulation should be installed in all exterior walls but it's even more important that you have it in the attic ceiling. A test of

You can save a good hunk on heating your house with plastic storm windows. You can get store-bought kits or just buy plastic and tape it over your windows. Plastic is just as good as having storm windows.

wall insulation is to observe the ground after a snowfall has settled: If there are bare spots, it means heat is escaping, melting the snow. The inside of exterior walls may also feel cold if insulation is inadequate or nonexistent. Also, observe the roof. If snow is missing in spots, it means heat is escaping and insulation is inadequate. Again, the most important place for insulation is in the attic—it can cut heating costs 40 percent.

HOUSE CAULKING

Apply caulking to all the "seams" of the house: doors and windows and where dissimilar materials meet, such as where the foundation walls meet siding. Caulk keeps heat from escaping. If seams are extra wide, save more money by first filling them with oakum, a ropelike material available at hardware stores. Then finish with caulk.

USE WEATHERSTRIPPING TO HELP KEEP HEAT IN

Weatherstripping is the stuff you use inside the house around doors and windows to seal gaps and prevent heat from escaping there. While those gaps may not seem like much, collectively they can add up to a hole your son could drive a toy Mack truck through. There are a variety of weatherstrip products available, both temporary and permanent. Temporary weatherstrips include ropelike caulk that you press into gaps; vinyl strips tacked in place are more permanent.

SEAL ALL OPENINGS

Think about how heat can escape from your house, then plug up all the openings. For example, close the fireplace damper and spaces around your air conditioner (even better, remove it and close the window if the machine is of that type). Always seal openings to your attic, around pipes, loose doors, stairways, light fixtures, and cracks of any kind.

Look for the Energy Star Label on All Products

As we mentioned before, you can save a lot of energy by buying products with the Energy Star label, such as computers and televisions. Yet you might be surprised to see this label on other products, such as windows and metal roofing. And new products are certain to be added in the future. So always look for the Energy Star label when buying just about any appliance, electrical device, or home construction or home improvement product.

GET IN THE HABIT OF USING ENERGY EFFICIENTLY

Little things can mean a lot when it comes to saving energy. And once you get into the habit, it's easy.

KEEP PILOT LIGHTS REGULATED

If you have a gas stove, keep the pilot light properly regulated. It can waste a tremendous amount of gas. Turn the dial until the flame is all blue with a little yellow at its top.

COVER HEATING ELEMENTS

When you're cooking something on the stove, use a pot or pan that covers the heating element completely so heat doesn't escape.

USE STOVE WHENEVER POSSIBLE

Whenever you can, cook something on the stove rather than in the oven. A stove uses a lot less fuel than an oven.

DISTRIBUTE CLOTHES PROPERLY IN DRYER

When drying clothes, dry all the lighter items separately from the heavy garments. Light clothes take less time to dry, so there's no sense mixing them into the longer-drying heavy garments.

WASH DISHES ALL AT ONCE

Store dirty dishes in the machine during the day and wash them all at once. It allows the machine to work at peak efficiency.

DON'T USE THE DRY CYCLE IN DISHWASHER

A dishwasher uses the most electricity during the dry cycle. You needn't use it. Just let the dishes air dry.

WASH CLOTHES IN COLD WATER

As much as possible, wash clothes in cold water, using cold water detergent. Doing this saves on electricity and the fuel needed by your hot water heater.

PULL WINDOW DRAPERIES SHUT

Closing your draperies at night helps impede the flow of warm air out through the window glass. But during the day, keep draperies open. This lets the sun in and helps warm the room.

FIX FAUCETS

Dripping faucets waste a surprising amount of water and, if it's hot water, they waste energy, too, because the hot water heater has to keep working to keep water in the tank hot.

DRAIN YOUR HOT WATER HEATER

Drain off the sediment that collects in bottom of water tank once every month. This allows it to work more efficiently.

CLEAN RADIATORS

Use a vacuum to keep the radiators free of dust. This keeps hot air flowing freely.

KEEP FURNITURE AWAY FROM RADIATORS

Big, heavy furniture should not be located in front of radiators. This make it harder for heat to reach areas of room where it's most needed.

MAKE SURE HEATING REGISTERS ARE OPEN

If you have a forced-warm-air heating system, make sure the registers are open. They could have been closed accidentally.

REPLACE THE FURNACE FILTER

Another good thing to do with a forced-warm-air system is to replace the filter when required, or clean it. It's located at the mouth of the main duct to the furnace. Vacuum it on both sides, then hold it up to the light. If light passes through, it's clean; if not, get a new one at the hardware store.

"BLEED" RADIATORS

If you have a hot-water heating system, every now and then open the valve located at the end of the radiator, either with a key provided by the manufacturer or a screwdriver. This bleeds off trapped air that interferes with heating. Hold a glass under the valve as you turn. When you hear a hissing noise, stop turning. As soon as the water runs it means the air pockets have been dissipated. Upstairs radiators are most likely candidates for this treatment.

TEST REFRIGERATOR GASKET

If you have a fairly old refrigerator, it may be that cold air is escaping because the gasket—the rubber stripping between the door and the refrigerator—is old and worn. This keeps the compressor going and wastes electricity. To test: Close the door on a single sheet of paper. If you can pull the paper out, you need a new gasket. Try the test all around the door because the gasket may have worn unevenly.

VACUUM UNDERNEATH REFRIGERATOR

Dust and dirt accumulate on the "works" beneath (and behind) the refrigerator and diminish its efficiency. Use your long, thin vacuum cleaner attachment and remove as much of this accumulation as you can—about twice a year, or more often.

CLOSE DOORS WHEN AIR CONDITIONER IS ON

If you have individual air conditioners in the rooms of your home, close the doors of those rooms. Otherwise, the units will work to cool an area larger than what they were designed for. This wastes electricity and diminishes cooling power.

KEEP FREEZER FILLED

To get the most for your money when using a freezer, keep it filled, use food from it often, and replace food quickly. If the freezer is filled twice instead of once a year, the operating cost per pound of stored food is only one-half as great. If you don't have enough food to fill the freezer put in bottles of water so that they will freeze.

Save $224 a Year— Small Savings Add Up

*A*ccording to *Popular Mechanics*, this is how much you can save by taking certain steps: only full loads of dishes and clothes washed = $51; water heater set at 120 degrees = $22; taking out room ACs in the cold weather = $40; using Energy Saving settings on all appliances = $21; washing clothes in cold water = $33; drying clothes on a clothesline when it's warm out = $57.

BUYING APPLIANCES

USE ENERGY-EFFICIENT APPLIANCES

- *Energy use can cost more over time than the cost of the appliance.*

It doesn't seem like a major consideration when you are looking at features and design, but the energy use of a new appliance is perhaps the most important consideration when purchasing an appliance. Indeed, you will spend more on the juice to run that appliance than you will to buy the product itself. Therefore, pick an energy-efficient model. According to the Federal Citizen Information Center, you should "look for the yellow Energy Guide label on products, and especially for products that have earned the government's ENERGY STAR®, which can save up to 50% in energy use." The Energy

Star (a U.S. government program) label is especially important since it assures you that the appliance or product is in compliance with U.S. government standards for energy efficiency.

What Is the Energy Star Standard?

*E*nergy Star is a standard for efficient energy use that was created in the United States by the Environmental Protection Agency but has now become an international standard. It is a voluntary program. An Energy Star label on a product means that it meets the highest standards for energy use. Originally a standard for computer products, the label is now on over forty thousand products with a variety of uses, everything from office equipment to windows. Always look for this label when buying anything that consumes or affects energy use. For more information go to www.energystar.gov.

FIGHT VAMPIRE ELECTRICITY WASTE

Many electrical devices draw electricity even when off, in what the industry calls standby mode. Called "vampire" energy suckers by critics, these devices consume a ton of electricity, even though you may not realize it. For this reason, use only Energy Star devices. You'll find Energy Star ratings for home electronics such as cordless phones, TVs, DVDs, battery charging systems, and home audio. As the Energy Star website states, "Home electronic products use energy when they're off to power features like clock displays and remote controls. U.S. households spend $100 per year to power devices while they are in this 'standby' power mode." As the Energy Star website in Australia states, "If your TV, VCR or DVD player complies with the ENERGY STAR standard, it will consume around 75% less energy in standby mode than standard products do. Because products like these spend more than 60% of their time on standby, this can add up to a significant reduction in energy use." In addition to these "vampire" savings, Energy Star home electronics use less energy than other devices, such as standard TVs. The Energy Star website states, "ENERGY STAR qualified TVs use about 30% less energy than standard units. You can find the ENERGY STAR on everything from standard TVs, to HD-ready TVs, to the largest flat-screen plasma."

CHECK WASHING MACHINE'S HOT WATER USE

Washing machines vary in the amount of hot water they use, from 15 to 25 gallons of water, roughly. Getting one that uses the least amount of water saves on water and the amount of energy needed to make hot water.

LARGE FREEZERS SAVE ON ENERGY

If you need the space, a larger freezer costs less to use per cubic foot. A larger freezer will use less energy than a smaller one. For example, the electricity to maintain 0 degrees Fahrenheit in a six-cubic-foot freezer for one day is 0.3 kilowatt hour per cubic foot, while an eighteen-cubic-foot size requires about 0.2 kilowatt hour per cubic foot per day.

Summary: Money-Saving Tips for Energy Use

- Fill oil tank in summer.
- Sign up for budget billing.

- Replace, repair, or clean your furnace.
- Get TOU rates.
- Lower the thermostat.
- Turn down the water heater.
- Get free energy audit.
- Get help from utility.
- Keep pilot light regulated.
- Use energy-efficient appliances.
- Cover heating element.
- Use stove whenever possible.
- Distribute clothes properly in dryer.
- Wash dishes all at once.
- Don't use dry cycle in dishwasher.
- Wash clothes in cold water.
- Install storm windows and doors.
- Install homemade storm windows.
- Install insulation.
- Use caulking to prevent heat loss.
- Use weatherstripping to prevent heat loss.
- Seal all openings to prevent heat loss.
- Pull window draperies shut.
- Fix faucets to stop loss of water and fuel.
- Drain sediment off bottom of water tank once a month.
- Clean radiators to increase functioning.
- Make sure heating registers are open.
- Replace filter to increase functioning.
- "Bleed" radiators to increase functioning.
- Test refrigerator gasket to make sure it's tight.
- Vacuum underneath refrigerator.
- Close doors when air conditioner is on.
- Check washing machine's hot water use.
- Large freezers save on energy.
- Keep freezer filled.

Chapter 8

FOOD AND GROCERIES

🛒

*T*he average family spends about $6,000 a year on groceries, but the plain and wonderful fact is that the average family can also lop thousands of dollars off that annual outlay without going on one of those crazed diets that show up in women's magazines every now and then in which one spends $25 a week to feed a family of six and where the core entrée is rice. You can, as the man says, have your cake and eat it, too.

HOW TO SAVE AT THE SUPERMARKET

BUY PRIVATE-LABEL ("STORE-BRAND") PRODUCTS

- *Save $1,800 a year per household buying store-brand foods.*

"Something many people don't know," says a supermarket manager friend of ours who will remain anonymous because he values his job, "is that national brand manufacturers such as Heinz and Wonder Bread produce quite a lot of foods under private labels for supermarkets." Indeed they do. Many big chains such as Stop & Shop, Pathmark, and Waldbaum's stock such products. Many people think the price difference between store and national brands is minuscule, only a few cents here and a few cents there. Not true. An independent research firm put together a varied market basket for the Private Label Manufacturers Association and compared prices of seventeen brand-name items with seventeen private-label products. It found a difference in price overall of about 25 percent. Rick did his own research with a local television crew. They went through a supermarket and put name brands in one basket and equivalent store brands in another. At checkout the name brands cost $45.61 while the store brands cost $26.72, a savings of about 40 percent. With the average household spending over $6,000 a year on groceries, the savings are substantial. For example, on ABC's *Good Morning America* a family bought only store brands for three weeks. They saved $108 during that period; on an annual basis the savings would be $1,872 per year.

And what's an even a bigger secret is that people in blind taste tests could not tell the difference between most store brands and national brands, as demonstrated some years back on ABC's *20/20*.

"If you are not familiar with store brands or private labels [the two terms mean the same]", our manager friend advises, "ask the manager of the supermarket where you shop for the brand names the store uses for its own products." For example, Wal-Mart has the Sam's Choice brand in the supermarket along with the Great Value product line, while Stop & Shop uses its own name and Waldbaum's has America's Finest.

You can switch from brand-name to private-label products gradually. To be fair, some national brands are tastier than store brands, so consumers should test out and compare each item. While this seems like a lot of trouble, it isn't. We recommend that a family buy two or three products of both the store brand and the national brand each time they go to the store, then give each product an unbiased test, preferably a blind test—but not too blind, as in "How's the spinach, honey?" "I don't know, I can't find it"—and then continue to buy those store brands when they can't find a difference or they have no

The store brand costs 89 cents, and the brand name Del Monte—
on sale—costs $1.31, a 42-cent difference! The difference in
quality, content, and taste—zero. Yearly savings buying store
brands can go as high as $1,800.

preference. If you buy some you don't like, just take them
back on your next regular trip to the store. Most stores are glad
to have you try their products and will offer a full money-back
guarantee, often printed on the product container. We'll bet
that you will like most of the store brands and won't mind putting an extra $1,000–$1,800 in your pocket.

BEWARE THE SIREN SONG OF THE SHELVES

National brands fight for their place on the shelves in the supermarket sun because it's so profitable. Through extensive
television and magazine advertising, they saturate unin-
formed consumers with the message that the extra cost of
their products is well worth the money. Their very visible marketing is combined with in-store paid product placement,
called "slotting fees," which allows them to place their prod-

Another trap: Supermarkets put stuff they want you to buy at eye level on the middle shelves and will often put stuff that kids like on the bottom shelves—at their eye level.

ucts on shelves that are at eye level, where customers can readily see and reach them, as opposed to shelves below the knees where they reach the eyes of kids (which can be expensive for parents) or on the top shelves where most shoppers don't readily look. In fact, the lower-priced products are usually in the top or bottom shelves (See "Avoiding the 'Nag Factor' "). Of course the consumer pays for all this marketing.

CHECK FOR FRESHNESS

Our manager friend also affirmed for us that supermarkets really "don't want you to know it, but they set up products and produce on shelves and the like so you'll grab the least fresh item." The big money-saving idea here is to for you take products from the back of the shelf or the display case. That's the way they're "packed out," as they say in the trade, because as the items in front are sold, items in back are added.

Hence getting the freshest vegetables and salads comes down to knowing that you should take from the back, and then double-checking freshness expiration dates on the packaging. Fresher food tastes better, lasts longer, and, the key point here, saves you money since you are more likely to avoid spoilage. We should emphasize this "last shall be first" selection process applies to many items in the store with short expiration dates, such as meat, milk, cheese and most other dairy products, as well as juice, chips, and bread.

THE BRAND-NAME MYTH

- *You pay a lot for a brand name, more than you may realize.*

You may not know it but you are paying a premium to buy brand-name products. All that advertising, packaging, promotions, shelf placement at stores, and dividends to shareholders costs money. And guess who pays for that? You do when you buy the product. Brand-name food at the grocery store, for example, can cost 20 percent and more than virtually the same product without all the hoopla.

Yet advertisers and marketers have managed to give brand names a kind of magic quality, a certain power that appears to separate them from "ordinary" goods. When your favorite sports hero wears Nike shoes or James Bond downs a vodka martini, it's hard not to want to grab a bit of that magic.

In addition, marketers have used two very powerful psychological motivators to cajole us into buying what they have to offer. These motivators are embarrassment and confidence. Many, many ads suggest that if you don't buy the product you might be embarrassed—think of the Sure deodorant ad and its slogan "Raise your hand if you are sure," which is a perfect example. On the one hand, if you don't buy the product, you might be embarrassed by underarm moisture; on the other hand, if you buy the product, you'll be confident and secure. At the deodorant company website (www.suredeodorant.com), the pitch goes even further: "Be Sure of Yourself," reads the main page. True, a lot of ads now are a bit less blatant, but they are just as manipulative. In fact, their less obvious nature makes them more dangerous because we probably don't recognize how they are trying to sway us. The point we are making is simple: Do you really want to go broke or into debt just to buy expensive brand-name goods that may be no better than much lower priced products that are virtually the same but lack a whole lot of hype?

We suggest that if you really want to save money, you learn to unhook yourself from the brand-name money pit and learn all the ways that you are being manipulated to pay more than you need to pay. Read on.

Trust Your Own Taste and Save a Bundle

*I*n a report titled "Does Premium Vodka's Taste Live Up to Its Price Tag?" ABC's 20/20 found that people often pay too much. Numerous people who favored a highly advertised, expensive vodka (with snob appeal) tried a variety of vodkas in a blind taste test. It turned out the most expensive vodka lost hands down when people did not know which brand they were drinking. Bottom line: Trust your taste and forget all that hype. You might save a bunch of money and get a better product to boot.

TIME IS MONEY—YOURS

> • *The longer you stay at a supermarket, the more you will spend.*

As *Consumer Reports* and others have reported, supermarkets are physically designed to slow your shopping experience, based on the simple and certainly correct calculation that the longer you stay, the more money you'll spend. Indeed, consumer reporter Janice Lieberman, in her book *Tricks of the Trade*, states, "It's estimated that every additional minute you're in a supermarket equals an extra dollar spent."

That is why your walk to get staples like milk or bread or meats may be fraught with the perils of candy, cake, snacks, and other temptations. So the advice is clear: Walk in, buy what's on your list—and do have a list—and depart.

Cut Down on Visits to the Supermarket

*E*very time you go into a supermarket you are subject to the temptation of buying something you don't necessarily need. Hence it's a good idea to limit the visits as much as you can, ideally to one big shopping visit a week. Experts say you can save over $100 a month, $1,200 a year.

WANT TO SAVE TIME AND MONEY? SHOP LATE

If you are a bit of a night owl and you're schedule will allow it, try shopping after regular hours. Many stores are open late, even twenty-four hours. For example, while Wal-Mart can be quite crowded from 9 AM to 6 PM, it is almost empty around

10 PM. As we pointed out in this book, the less time you stay in a store, the less money you spend. So shop late for a quick in/out—saving time and also money that you might have spent on impulse items.

THE INCREDIBLE SHRINKING PRODUCTS

Another exposé, as it were, of the supermarket is that many products are being downsized, and manufacturers are doing everything they can to keep you from noticing. *USA Today* reported that about "30% of packaged goods have lost content over the past year." For example, Hellman's mayonnaise has gone from 32 ounces to 30 ounces. Some cereal boxes have lost 1.5 ounces in the last year and of course in most cases the prices have not been downsized correspondingly. The good news is that 70 percent of supermarket products have not been downsized. Double-check contents before you buy. And if you notice a loss, for example in a cereal box you ordinarily would buy, look for boxes of the same type of cereal that give you more. And, as we detailed above, now might be a great time to try store brands and private labels.

BUY THE LARGE ECONOMY SIZE—NOT
  • *Some economy size products cost more
    than smaller sizes.*

For years consumers were exhorted by manufacturers that if they purchased the large economy size they would save money. This was true and made sense since large sizes require less packaging, less stocking, and the company gets more of your money up front. So why not settle for a smaller profit? "But those days," says ace shopper Anne Lundy of Huntington Station, New York, "are mostly gone with the wind. But I've found it pays to check the unit price labels on the shelves. Lots of people will be shocked because I've discovered that many items are more expensive in the large, economy sizes." Lundy adds, "They really try to baloney you because they'll have words plastered across a package such as *Value Pack*. That's just a lie, since it implies that it's selling at a bargain price." Lundy is right on.

For example, at our local Wal-Mart, we found the following prices for tuna fish:

Chunk light tuna:
6-ounce can = 13.7 cents per ounce
12-ounce can = 16 cents per ounce

Albacore tuna:
6-ounce can = 21.4 cents per ounce
12-ounce can = 23 cents per ounce

Ketchup and peanut butter also can be more expensive in large sizes. We have also seen this price discrepancy in a variety of other products such as toilet paper, tampons, and tissues. Double-check that unit price. And if there is no unit price listed, you can always do your own calculation with a handheld calculator.

ARE COUPONS WORTH CLIPPING?

We don't recommend a lot of couponing at supermarkets for people who have not done that on a regular basis before. The reason is that you'll do a lot better buying store brands. Of course we also know that, at the same time, some people can do very well with coupons. But if you've never done serious couponing before—even though you may have seen those TV stories where the housewife checks out with a full basket of groceries and only pays ten dollars—just realize that couponing is a lot of work and it's rarely as lucrative every week as is shown in those TV demonstrations.

Revenue magazine, a marketing trade publication, reported that "overall coupon redemption rates hover between 1 and 3 percent year-over-year." This means that in any given year 97 percent of people (some years 99 percent) are not heavy coupon users. So there must be a reason. *Promo,* another trade magazine, went on to say that redemption rates were at 2 percent in good times and about 2.5 percent in bad times but "the growth [in bad times] isn't generated so much by an influx of new clippers as it is from increased activity among committed users." The magazine noted that coupons have been getting more complicated recently: "Multiple-purchase requirements [for redeeming a coupon] were employed in 24 percent of all programs," meaning that a quarter of today's coupons require two or more purchases and are therefore more of a hassle.

Don't Just Look for Food Coupons

*I*f you like to use coupons, these days there are a variety of ways to get them on the cheap. According to the *Reader's Digest,* there are coupons available for purchasing clothing, restaurants, even movies. (Go to www.retailmenot.com.) For example, as the magazine says, if your family eats out "twice a month at $75 a meal you'll save $180 a year if you use coupons worth a ten percent discount."

BE ALERT TO SCANNING MISTAKES

There are ordinarily no prices on products anymore, so we have to accept, more or less on faith, that the checkout scanner is accurately ringing up the right amount every time we shop at the supermarket. Yet this is hardly always the case.

The county of San Bernardino in California reported in 2003 that "a statewide survey revealed that shoppers were overcharged on more than 2 percent of items" due to scanning errors.

The term *scanning error* is actually a misnomer. The scanner scanned correctly, but the correct price was not put into the database that the scanner accessed. This usually happens when a price is changed, and most price changes are due to

To really save, get used to comparing unit prices on supermarket items. Unit price measures, as it were, apples against apples.

sales. In other words, sale prices are not entered as they should be. Eliminating most scanning errors is simple enough. Place your sale items at the back of your cart and put them last in line on the belt—and keep an eagle eye on them as they are scanned. If there is an error, it is bound to be at this point. "Sometimes," says shopper Chris Vano, "mistakes are also made with nonsale items, but ninety-something percent of the time I've found it's when sale prices are involved."

If you do spot an error, many stores will give you the item free or give you a coupon for a free item or refund you more than the pricing error. Overcharging a customer is bad for the store's image and may even be illegal. So if you find you were overcharged, be insistent. At this point, most stores will bend over backward to please you. It is also a very good idea to correct a price before the transaction is completed, because after that it can really be a hassle, involving a refund and paperwork. You can, of course, check the receipt—if you suspect you were overcharged, do it as soon as possible.

Speaking of errors, listen to what Jim Dolan of Comsewogue, New York, said: "Every time my wife, Mary, went into the supermarket, she kept noticing that the prices being rung up on her vegetables and fruits were quite different each time. She investigated and she discovered that produce doesn't have bar codes! So the clerk has to look up the price for each type of produce—and much of the time they got the price wrong. She didn't think they were trying to cheat her. It was just that one kind of tomato looks pretty much like another, especially when the clerk is under siege with dozens of people waiting on line." The Dolans found a good way to handle the problem. "Now," Jim says, "every time she buys produce she first writes down or remembers the price so that when the store clerk rings it up, she can immediately question the price."

SPECIFIC FOOD TIPS

MAKE THAT GREAT CUP OF COFFEE FOR PEANUTS

- *It's not the brand of coffee you buy but how you make it that matters.*

What would you pay for a perfect cup of coffee? Gourmet beans and all? Ten dollars a pack, fifteen dollars a pack? How about three dollars a pack? Everyone says Rick makes the best coffee, and he always uses low-priced, store-brand, 100 percent Columbian coffee beans for three bucks a pack. And he uses an inexpensive Mr. Coffee coffeemaker (from $15 to $20) to do the job.

The most important trick to making a good cup of coffee is not expensive beans but rather how you make it. Careful measuring is the key. When you get it exactly right, coffee has that richness and aroma that we all crave. First measure the coffee carefully and then measure the water just as carefully. Be patient since it will probably take you a couple of tries before you get it right. If the coffee is too strong or a bit bitter, add more water or use less coffee the next time. If the drink is weak or does not have much taste, use less water or add more coffee. Once you get it right, make a note of the exact measurements of water and coffee and use that same measurement each time. Rick believes that just a couple of tablespoons of water can make a big difference.

However, if you change brands of coffee, you'll have to go through that trial-and-error process again to find the right measurements for that particular brand.

So how much will this save you? If you go through a pound of coffee a week you might save $4 using a store brand instead of a moderately priced gourmet brand. And $4 a week would add up to about $200 a year in savings.

So wake up and smell the coffee.

Buy Some Foods in Bulk

Somehow, health food stores have an image of being expensive. But you can save money by buying some foods there in bulk—foods that you can't get in supermarkets. The manager of one store says, "For example, oatmeal can be bought in large sizes and it's cheaper and fresher than your best brand names. Also rice, nuts, flour, many other things."

HEALTH FOOD: BUY IT BY THE CASE, SAVE 10 PERCENT

Unlike most supermarkets, some health food stores will also sell you many foods by the case and at good discounts (10 percent at the ones we checked). You can get canned vegetarian items, oils, jellies, and cookies. Some other products available include honey, syrup, candy, vegetables, and cider vinegar. Some items, say cider vinegar, may be available in cases with more items than you need. In this instance, ask if the store will split the case in half and still give you a discount.

USE A WATER FILTER
- *Filter your tap water; it may be as good as bottled!*

Twenty-five percent of bottled water comes from city water supplies, according to shopping expert Phil Lempert of NBC. While many bottled waters are from springs, a large number are just plain tap water. So you might be paying megabucks to haul water from a store that you could get more easily from your own faucet. How were you fooled? Simple: The label often shows pictures of mountains, tall pine trees, and bubbling brooks. But these picture are meaningless. If the label does not specifically state that the source is spring water, you should be suspicious.

We think that most people can save a ton of money by drinking water from the tap and filtering it themselves if they want to increase the quality. A simple gravity-fed Brita water pitcher can remove lead and other impurities for much less money and with greater certainty than buying tap water from another city. The pitcher with the first filter costs about $12 initially. Additional filters are about $5 each and are good for forty gallons (about 12 cents per gallon).

ICE

- *Buy ice in bulk.*

Like other things, you can buy ice cubes in bulk. If you can locate the ice cube distributor (try "Ice" in the yellow pages) you can buy large bags (forty-five pounds) for half of what you'd pay in a store. However, some convenience stores also carry some of these big bags. These can be stored in your freezer, if not used up at one large party.

CHILDREN AND FOOD

CHILDREN ARE PAYING A LOT TO GAIN A LOT: BAD DAY AT McDONALD'S

Our children are getting the hard sell. Food marketers are targeting them deliberately while many parents seem unaware of the advertising pressures that their children have been subjected to. The food that these kids eat is expensive in the short term and very expensive in the long term since they could suffer from obesity for the rest of their lives. This unhealthy food can also lead to an early onset of diabetes.

Food makes up a very large category of advertising on TV shows aimed at kids. These ads feature bowls brimming with cereal, overstuffed sandwiches, and youngsters happily gulping down humongous drinks. The package design of these products often displays a favorite cartoon character.

The hard sell continues at the supermarket. What parent has not been nagged by a child to buy a certain toaster pastry or candy? These highly advertised products are often placed on the shelves at child's eye level so that a son or daughter will see the brightly colored package pitched on TV and nag parents until they buy (known as the "nag factor" by consumer watchers).

But is this just conjecture? *USA Today* stated that Yale University psychology professor Kelly Brownell said, "One study found that the average American child sees 10,000 TV food ads a year, mostly for sugar-laden foods, fast foods and soft drinks." A study done at the University of North Carolina at Chapel Hill looked at government data dealing with 21,000 children from two to eighteen years old during the time period of 1977 to the mid-1990s. They discovered that young people in recent years were getting 25 percent of their calories from sugary, fattening snacks versus 18 percent in 1977. All this adds up to about 150 extra calories a day.

Recent studies now are beginning to prove conclusively that such marketing and advertising are bad for our kids. For example, Commercial Alert, a nonprofit organization, reports, "Research into the dietary and viewing habits of more than 162,000 children in 35 countries has revealed that their consumption of sweets and fizzy drinks rises with each hour they spend in front of the box. By contrast, the amount of fresh fruit and vegetables falls."

Parents need to take back control of their children's eating habits. And parents need to be aware that children are bombarded by forces outside the family, forces that may lead to an overweight lifestyle. Parents need to talk with their children about the consequences of bad eating habits—after all, no child wants to be seen as "fat." A parent might even tape a children's program and, with the child at the parent's side, critique the ads, showing how they deceive and manipulate children.

Avoiding the "Nag Factor"

Kids bugging Mom or Dad to buy things in the supermarket is known in the trade as the "nag factor." To avoid this irritant, we suggest you affix them with blindfolds, leave them home, or take your medication before you go to the supermarket.

"FRUIT DRINK" BEVERAGES: EXPENSIVE AND UNHEALTHY

Not only are children being sold expensive brand-name foods that they nagged their parents to buy, but these foods often are not what they claim to be and are very bad for a child's health. So save money, and don't buy 'em.

For example, Little Hug, is a "fruit drink" for very small children and packaged in cute little plastic containers. Now if you've read this far, you might not think you would be surprised by any manufacturer's deception, but this one really does take the top prize, so hold on to your seat. Little Hug "fruit drink" contains no fruit juice. That's right, zero. It does, however, contain water, sugar, and 60 calories.

We failed to locate any nutritional information at the website of the Little Hug manufacturer, the American Beverage Corporation. Instead we had to find a carton of the stuff and then look carefully at the required federal label on the side of the box. Yet on its website the company proudly announces, "Since 1985, we have sold more than 8 billion HUGS, that's more bottles of kids' drinks than anyone else in the world! These drinks are available in a variety of delicious flavors and packaging options including the newly redesigned Little Hug 6-pack and 24ct Assorted featuring Hug Man!"

Summary: Money-Saving Tips for Supermarkets

- Gradually try store brands over national brands.
- Buy the freshest products you can so spoilage is less likely.
- Be aware of downsized products.
- Be wary of buying large economy sizes.
- Remember that products are placed on shelves to entice you to buy.
- Don't stay in the store a long time. Time means your money!
- Beware scanning errors on sales items.
- Beware scanning errors on produce that looks alike.
- Beware marketing to children of unhealthy, expensive foods.

Chapter 9

GARDEN SUPPLIES

SALES AND DISCOUNTS

CHECK NURSERIES FOR SEASONAL SALES

Nurseries often run seasonal sales on just about everything they have—plants, flowers, you name it. While you will find sales during the regular season, the best time to buy is generally in the off-season.

SHOP NURSERIES AND OUTLETS FOR AFTER-CHRISTMAS SALES

Garden supply outlets are very competitive with other kinds of stores on after-Christmas items, with prices slashed 50 percent or more.

DON'T ASSUME SMALL NURSERIES HAVE HIGHER PRICES

It is true that supermarkets offer better prices than the local delicatessens, but this isn't necessarily the case with large nurseries, which have tremendous overhead. For example, a check of artificial Christmas trees at a small outlet showed a $62.99 price tag there and $69.99 at a large chain-type outlet.

BEWARE BUYING ON-SALE TREES

When a tree is on sale, make certain that it's good—you could end up fertilizing it with a lot of money and it still won't grow. If a tree comes with a root ball, the ball should be compact and unbroken and have, as one professional landscaper says, "one foot of ball for every one inch diameter of tree trunk."

GARDEN SUPPLIES

BUY PEAT MOSS IN LARGE SIZES

You can get a good buy on peat moss if you buy it in the largest quantities. The larger the size, the more you can save, up to around 25 percent.

BUY UNWRAPPED PEAT POTS

If you need some peat pots, stay away from the kind that are nicely wrapped in cellophane or the like and come in groups. Ones sold loose by dealers are a lot cheaper. Reason: The dealer buys the pots in bulk at low cost and then transfers the savings to you in the retail price.

Get Guaranteed Shovels and Hoes

Two garden implements that take a lot of abuse are shovels and hoes—and they've been known to break. Many brands are not guaranteed. So, buy only ones that are guaranteed, so you can get your money back if the implement breaks.

FERTILIZER AND INSECTICIDES

BUY FERTILIZER IN LARGE SIZES

This is another product that you can save on by buying in quantity rather than as you need it. For example, if you have a 5,000-square-foot area to fertilize you could buy 5,000 square feet of fertilizer for each of the three times (or whatever is required in your area) needed, but you'd pay a premium price for each batch. Better buy the largest size usable. The largest size is for 15,000 square feet; buying it would save $3 to $4. Fertilizer will keep nicely.

USE CHEMICAL FERTILIZER IN SPRING AND FALL

There are basically three types of fertilizer: chemical and organic, and a mixture of the two. The higher the organic content, the more you pay. Check when it's best to use what in your area. For example, on Long Island, New York, you can use an all-chemical fertilizer in the spring and fall and not risk "burning"—browning and perhaps killing—the lawn. If you can use chemical rather than organic, you may be able to save some money.

RESIST THE IMPULSE TO BUY INSECTICIDE IN BULK

Unlike with many products, buying insecticide in large amounts really doesn't pay because you use only small amounts at one time. Meanwhile, as one pro puts it, "the rest of it sits around for a long time." Incidentally, take great care where you store chemicals, especially if kids are around.

LAWNS

BUY GRASS SEED SUITED TO YOUR AREA

A mistake many people make is to buy the best—and most expensive—seed available. "They get Merion Blue Grass in the mistaken belief that the best seed will do the best job on their lawn. But that seed in a shady area or moist area may end up looking terrible," says one expert. Save money and problems by suiting the seed to your particular job.

GET A DISCOUNT ON LOOSE GRASS SEED

You can save money buying grass seed by buying it loose. Large feed and grain outlets carry it loose and will mix it to your specifications—or sell you the "components" and you can mix it yourself. If you're not certain what you need, the dealer—and let's hope he's honest—can advise you.

DON'T BUY UNNEEDED BULK GRASS SEED

Though there are sales on grass seeds, it is generally a standard price. Buying it in bulk will only save you a dollar or two, but there's a danger. If you don't use it fairly fast, the seed will deteriorate, losing about 10 percent of its viability in a year. It's really better to buy what you need at the moment and use it right away.

STAY AWAY FROM "AUTOMATED" LAWN MAINTENANCE SERVICES

Professional gardening men advise that engaging one of those lawn maintenance firms that come in to power-roll, aerate, and chemically maintain (they don't cut the grass) a lawn is a good way to get ripped off. Their fees are often double, triple, or more of what a professional landscaper would charge, and what they do is simple. "You could do a better job aerating with spiked golf shoes," says one professional. As far as applying chemicals—fertilizer, weed killers, etc.—they don't do it necessarily at the right time to do any good. Moreover, applying seed willy-nilly to a lawn doesn't do any good. The soil has to be prepared for the seed, and they don't do that. "The reason people pay the high price," he goes on to explain, "is because the big machines look as if something important is happening to their lawns." Solution: Aerate and apply chemicals yourself, or have an individual professional do it.

A SOD LAWN MAY BE CHEAPER THAN A SEED LAWN

Most people think of a sod lawn as being more expensive than a seed lawn. But if you live in an area where seed lawns are hard to establish—rain keeps washing seed away, for instance—aborted seed-lawn attempts can run into more money than it costs to put in sod. So shop around, get prices on sod, and seriously consider it. One pro advises, "If you have it done by a pro, it can cost you double and more than double what a seed lawn would in original cost, but it is something a do-it-yourselfer can manage." He also says that "a lot of professionals tend to rip off people when installing lawns by either method—sod or seed."

Summary: Money-Saving Tips for Garden Supplies

- Don't assume small nurseries have higher prices.
- Things go on sale at nurseries after Christmas.
- Beware buying on-sale trees; they may not be good.
- Check nurseries for seasonal sales.

- Buy peat moss in large sizes.
- Buy unwrapped peat pots—they're cheaper than wrapped.
- Buy guaranteed shovels and hoes.
- Buy fertilizer in large sizes.
- Use chemical fertilizer in spring and fall; it can work better than organic.
- Don't buy insecticide in bulk; much can go to waste.
- Don't buy grass seed in bulk; it can deteriorate quickly.
- Buy grass seed suited to your area, not the best grass seed.
- Don't hire lawn maintenance outfits; they may rip you off.
- Sod lawn is sometimes cheaper than seed lawn.

Chapter 10

HARDWARE

🛒

As with other categories, there are good ways to save on hardware. Following is a roundup.

DISCOUNTS ARE AVAILABLE ON EVERYTHING FROM LUMBER TO TOILETS

- *Haggle for a lower cost.*

Do your homework on cost, which includes shopping around—and then use the haggling tips in the Shopping Tip #2 section to get the discount you want. As with other items, the higher the price, the easier it will be to haggle. In fact, if an item costs only a few dollars, you won't be able to haggle because the profit margin is so slim. However, if the item gets to about $30 or so, then let the haggling commence. And as the figure fattens, so will the size of the discount.

CARDED ITEMS COST MUCH MORE THAN LOOSE

More than ever, companies are packaging items in so-called carded form, a piece of cardboard with the product retained by some sort of clear plastic blister. In general, such items cost 25 percent more than items you'd buy loose, but it can get ridiculous. One of us saw some stove bolts for sale in a hardware store for $1.83 while the same number of bolts loose sold for 21 cents.

Hence the idea is to buy loose whenever you can: nails, screws, bolts, whatever. While the trend in marketing today is toward carded, there are still outlets—particularly hardware stores—where you can get things loose. All you have to do is pick up the phone and call.

YOU CAN GET DISCOUNTS FROM ALL KINDS OF OUTLETS

Discounts can be found at home centers and plumbing and electrical supply stores (once the exclusive province, discount-wise, of the pros). Every single retailer we talked with when we were researching hardware and home improvement said they gave discounts. The reason is simple: It's good business.

BUYING IN BULK IS NOT ALWAYS BEST

Most of the time things sold in bulk will save you money. For example, the more screws and nails you buy, the more you'll save per pound. But the key point is this: Unless you use it all, you can lose. Years ago, before Tom learned this lesson, he went into a plumbing supply store to get a washer for a leaky faucet. So when he asked the proprietor for a washer, the man asked Tom, "Box of one hundred?"

"Sure," Tom said.

Tom's question now is this: Anyone interested in buying a small box containing ninety-seven flat red washers?

Store-Brand Hardware Items

*A*s we have recommended throughout this book, store-brand products are often much cheaper and a very good deal. Hardware stores are carrying more and more of these each year.

SHOP AROUND

Comparison shopping really pays off with hardware and home improvement. On some things—tools, particularly—you can also check various catalogs. We've gotten some winners with great prices, and you can use them as a sort of benchmark for your shopping.

You must know what you're buying because you can't get a bargain on an item unless you know what you are purchasing when comparing prices. For example, many manufacturers make many different look-alike models of toilets, siding, and other products. Your safest bet is to find out what the model number is.

Get the Store to Break Open a Package

*S*ome stores will break open packages to sell a limited number of items. Most hardware stores will break open packages of popular items. For example, if you need a single caster or fuse the proprietor might break open a package of two or four. If you just need one or two of an item, this saves you money. This can keep the rest of the items from going to waste, as it were.

Summary: Money-Saving Tips for Hardware

- Almost all hardware items may be gotten at discount.
- Carded items cost a lot more than loose.
- Buying in bulk is not always wise.
- Shop around.
- Some stores will break open packages to sell single items.

Chapter 11

HEALTH CARE

*I*n 2008 the Commonwealth Fund, a well-respected charitable foundation that specializes in health-care issues, released a report that found the following: U.S. health-care quality fell from fifteenth in the world to nineteenth while the United States spent more money than any other country on health care. The report found that the system was inefficient, with patients having to wait much longer to see a doctor than those in other countries, yet at the same time U.S. citizens paid more money due to "high insurance administrative costs."

Happily, though, despite its overall problems, there are methods one can use to make, as it were, healthy cuts in the costs of health care, including costs for doctors and even hospitals. Following are some tips.

HOW TO LOWER HEALTH-CARE COSTS

BUY HEALTH INSURANCE WITH A HIGH DEDUCTIBLE

- *A high deductible can save you as much as 40 percent in premiums.*

A high deductible can save you a bundle while at the same time providing coverage for catastrophic problems—the kinds that are life-threatening or could send your family into bankruptcy. A deductible of $7,500 could save you as much as 40 percent over insurance with a lower deductible. And there are ways, as detailed later, of reducing those out-of-pocket expenses.

In addition, just having health insurance, even with a high deductible, has many other benefits. For example, some clinics won't deal with patients who have no insurance. Having a policy means that even though you may have to pay the clinic out of your own pocket, you will get the care you need.

OPEN A GOVERNMENT HEALTH INSURANCE ACCOUNT (HSA)
  • *Put money into a tax-free account.*

Let's suppose that you have health insurance with a high deductible, as suggested above, and so can put pretax money into a tax-free account (up to $3,000 for an individual, $5,950 for a family), which you can then access for medical expenses that are not paid for by the policy. In addition, the savings will roll over year after year and any money that accumulated could be taken out for any reason with no penalty after retirement. Or funds could be taken out early for any reason with only a few penalties. Now wouldn't that make sense? You would be paying much less for health insurance, dealing with less paperwork, setting money aside for expenses not covered, and, if you managed to save money in this account, you could keep it.

Well, such a thing does exist. A health savings account (HSA) does exactly that and is a U.S. government program. It is available to people who are enrolled in a high-deductible health plan (HDHP). We think it is one of the best ideas since sliced bread; the odds are that you could save a considerable amount in this account. In fact you could consider the HSA to be a kind of retirement fund. You can read a full description at the U.S. Treasury website: http://www.ustreas.gov/offices/public-affairs/hsa.

Just Ask!

When a doctor billed Rick an amount above what his insurance would cover for a medical procedure, he asked the doctor to accept only what his insurance would pay as payment in full. The doctor did this with no fanfare whatsoever; Rick just had to ask.

HAGGLE OVER HEALTH-CARE COSTS—IT WORKS

Whether you have an HSA or not, you still have tools that you can use to reduce your expenses that are not covered by your high-deductible health insurance policy.

The first tool is to haggle. A 2002 Harris Interactive poll found that even though only 17 percent of people haggle over health-care costs, doctors and others are willing to bargain. Of those in the poll who did haggle with their doctors, 54 percent were successful; of those who haggled with a hospital, 45 percent were successful.

Gerard Anderson, the director of the Johns Hopkins Center for Hospital Finance and Management, said, "If you go into the hospital and ask the chief financial officer, you may get a 30 percent discount, but you have to ask for it. It's totally up to the discretion of the CFO how much they or the person in the billing office are willing to give you."

Ask and You Shall Receive

*J*ake Bowen of Birmingham, Alabama, got a hospital bill for $805 that his insurance, which had a high deductible, didn't eliminate. He said, "I called the hospital to see what I could do." With very little trouble they put Jake on a plan, where he paid off the bill at $25 a month but with no interest. "In essence," he said, "I got a free loan and saved about three years' worth of interest charges."

DON'T PAY THE DOCTOR RIGHT AWAY

Even if you know that the cost of a visit will come out of your pocket because you have high-deductible health insurance, don't pay your doctor right away. With a high deductible, you will, almost certainly, have to pay most minor expenses, but

	Billed	Not owed due to agreement with insurance	Owed by patient	Savings
Lab	$38	$12	$26	32%
Doctor's bill	$75	$28	$47	37%
Total	$113	$40	$73	35%

your insurance may have an agreement with your health-care providers that puts a cap on the costs that you must pay.

Your best plan is to have your doctor or hospital bill your insurance company. When you and your doctor hear back from the insurance company, this form should spell out clearly just what expenses you must pay and how much—prices that are often much less than the doctor billed initially. For example, here are typical savings that Rick found when he was billed by a lab and by a doctor.

"BALANCE BILLING"—A MEDICAL BILLING SCAM

BusinessWeek reported on its investigation of an often illegal practice by hospitals, labs, doctors, and health-care service providers in billing patients for expenses over and above what the patient's insurance company paid.

In "balance billing," patients are often hit with an extra bill after they thought their insurance company had paid all their costs. And to add insult to injury, many health-care companies that send out such bills use bill-collecting agencies to threaten the patients.

Confused and uncertain, many patients end up paying huge amounts, often thousands of dollars. Yet in most cases, these bills should be going to the insurer and not to the patient. And in a significant number of cases, these bills are scams. Bottom line: If you have medical treatment that was covered by your insurance, you should probably not pay any bills for that treatment that are addressed directly to you. Instead refer the company doing the billing back to your insurer and also notify your insurer since this billing is often a scam.

For Convenience,
See a "Doctor in a Box"

*A*s the Commonwealth Fund report cited earlier pointed out, Americans have to wait longer to see a doctor than people in other countries. For this reason, we recommend seeing a "doctor in a box" health service, the kind where you can just walk in with no appointment. For care that you would normally get from a general practitioner, these doctor-in-a-box outfits are well equipped and seem to be popping up just about everywhere. These independent and self-contained health-care businesses are often open early in the morning to late in the evening and on weekends. Look in your phone book for "urgent care" or walk-in general health-care services.

We have had very good luck with these for minor medical problems and we are usually in and out of the doctor's office in just an hour or so. In fact we like the service so much, we have given up seeing a regular family doctor and instead go almost exclusively to the doctor in a box when the occasion arises.

GET TREATED BY THE COUNTY YOU LIVE IN

One of the best-kept secrets in health care is that your county health department has a wide variety of free and inexpensive services. While many people think of these health departments as services for the poor, they are for everyone in the county. And some of the services are better than those that can be found anywhere else. For example, in our area the annual health exam was more thorough than a standard doctor exam but cost much less. Call your local health department and find out what services they offer.

Talk Money to Your Doctor

*W*e have found that doctors and other health-care professionals often do not know the price of the services they use. They might suggest that you have a lab test done, for example, but will not be able to tell you the cost of that test. We suggest that you be a bit forceful and insist on knowing the cost before committing to a test.

SAVE DOCTOR VISITS—KEEP A GOOD SET OF MEDICAL REFERENCES IN YOUR HOME

When Rick's wife began to run a high fever, he pulled out his two large home medical references and his prescription drug reference for information. These proved invaluable. While her fever was high, it was not dangerously high, as he determined from the book, so this meant they did not need to go immediately to the emergency room but could wait to see a doctor the next day. Further investigation revealed that she had been given the wrong medicine for her condition. The next day a trip to a doctor in a box got her the right medicine and she was on the road to recovery. (Of course, under no circumstances should you respond to a fever in an infant or young child by emulating Rick's response to his wife's high fever—that is, by checking a book to determine that a doctor's visit could be avoided for twenty-four hours.)

Having these references can save you a lot of money over time. They will help you avoid unnecessary trips to the doctor and also tell you when to seek help immediately, thus avoiding more costly treatment at a later date. Doctors have a saying about patients: Many who cannot be helped (such as those with the flu) go to a doctor for treatment, while others who should go to a doctor don't or wait too long, such as a person with a cut that has gotten infected.

Having medical references will help you determine the difference and save you a money and aggravation. Examples of such general references are the *American Medical Association Family Medical Guide* and *The Cornell Illustrated Medical Encyclopedia*. One drug reference is *The Essential Guide to Prescription Drugs*. (All of these books are available from Amazon.)

SHOP AROUND FOR A DENTIST

If you break your leg, you're not going to want to spend time comparison shopping; you'll want to get your leg attended to ASAP! However, other medical costs can be compared. For example, if you must get a crown on one of your teeth, you can shop around. Dr. David Robertson of Morehead City, North Carolina, said, "Dental expenses are fairly predictable," which makes comparing the cost of one dentist to another pretty straightforward. And while you should of course not shop only for price, cost *is* a good place to start. After putting together a list of possible dentists and their pricing, ask your friends about their experiences with the doctors you are considering. Then choose the one with a good reputation who has the lowest cost.

SPORTS AND EXERCISE

DON'T SIGN A LONG-TERM CONTRACT WITH A HEALTH CLUB

In the past the health club industry has required long-term contracts, some of which were very deceptive. In addition, some health clubs went bankrupt, which meant that people who had paid money up front were out of luck. If you must sign a long-term contract, ask a lot of questions. Health clubs have a reputation for hiding extra fees and requirements in mice-size type. For example, they often include an "initiation fee" in addition to the stated price. Some plans allow you to use the club only on certain days.

If you need to use a health club and you have a choice, shop around. The AARP suggests you ask the following questions: "Does the club have a month-to-month contract? Some clubs are doing away with yearly contracts and going to monthly ones to attract members." You can also look for a pay-per-day facility. The Maryland attorney general's office stated that, in Maryland at least, these clubs "charge for their services only on a pay-as-you-go basis. They do not charge any initiation fees or up front fees, and may not charge for more than one day's services at any time."

Pay-per-Day Option at Many Health Clubs

If you live out of town (a vague term if there ever was one), some health clubs will let you pay by the day. In the area where Rick lives, for example, he can use several health clubs on a one-day basis since he lives out in the country. He's considered a "visitor" by the health clubs and therefore the rules are different.

LIFESTYLE EXERCISE: CHEAP, EASY, AND HEALTHY

To save money on exercise equipment, a great solution is not to buy but instead to adjust your lifestyle so that you have exercising built into it. Lifestyle exercise means that you take the stairs instead of the elevator. You park at the back of the parking lot and walk a ways—which also means that you will always be able to find a parking space. You walk to the lunch restaurant at noon or go to the park to eat your bagged lunch. Even vacuum cleaning or mopping or cleaning out your garage adds to your exercise total. But it can be fun, too. Dance, frolic with the kids, play catch—be creative. Any exercise will add to your lifestyle total.

The added benefit is that it is actually easier to work this kind of exercise into what you do every day than to try to set aside an hour each day or so for an exercise routine. Tom, who had bypass surgery, walks thirty-five to forty minutes extra every day, "and the last time the doctor looked at my arteries she said they were 'beautiful.' It's been a long time since anyone called any part of me beautiful!"

HAGGLE OVER HEALTH CLUB FEES

Health clubs were once booming (in the late nineties there were 70 million "echo boomers"), but now growth has slowed severely. So the time is ripe to join, and the best time is the end of August, when sales personnel are trying to make their sales goals in a traditionally slow month. Quoted in 2008 in *Money* magazine, Spencer Ellis, president of the National Exercise & Sports Trainers Association, said, "Tell them straight up that price is an important factor for you, and ask what wiggle room there might be on rates." *Money* magazine went on to say, "You're most likely to score a break on initiation fees (which typically run $100 to $285), but you may be able to get a deal on monthly fees (usually $40 to $80) too." If you're already a member of a club, you should keep an eye peeled for club promotions from its competitors. If you see a lower rate, request that the club match it.

TRADE IN SPORTS EQUIPMENT AND/OR BUY USED

Kids can outgrow sports gear in a year. Instead of letting it pile up in your garage, where it will just go to waste, why not trade it in and get a credit for any new gear you might need? One chain store in particular specializes in swaps and sells both used and new equipment. Play It Again Sports has more than four hundred locations across the country. To find a store near you go to their website, www.playitagainsports.com.

As the company's website says, "There are thousands of parents right in your hometown whose kids participate in all kinds of sports. That translates into an enormous inventory of equipment and gear—most of which has plenty of great seasons left in it. Instead of getting pennies on the dollar for this valuable merchandise in a garage sale, savvy parents like you have discovered they can save big on sporting goods by trading up at Play It Again Sports."

Parents and adults can take advantage of this service for themselves as well. If you are just starting a sport, take our advice: Buy used equipment and save a bundle of money. A used set of golf clubs will cost a lot less than a new set. Many people buy a ton of equipment only to lose interest after spending money on gear that they'll never use. The solution is to buy used when possible and then sell or trade in equipment that no longer interests you.

GET INFOMERCIAL SPORTS EQUIPMENT FOR A SONG

You can also buy exercise equipment as seen on infomercials on TV at a substantial discount. The odds are that you can also find used stuff like that. In fact, many people who order those rarely if ever use them. Many end up in the closet and then get sold for peanuts. Check the local classifieds to see what's for sale and also Craigslist.com.

Summary: Money-Saving Tips for Health Care

- Buy insurance with high deductible to save greatly on premiums.
- Open a health savings account (HSA).
- Haggle over health-care fees.
- Don't pay doctor right away.
- Avoid balance billing.
- Get treated by county you live in.
- Buy medical references.
- Shop around for dentist—prices vary for same service.
- Don't sign long-term health club agreement.
- Get exercise through the way you live.
- Haggle over health club fees to save on fitness equipment.

Chapter 12

HOLIDAY EXPENSES

"The average consumer expects to shell out $763 on gifts" for Christmas, according to *USA Today*. During the holiday season, stores pull out their full bag of tricks to get us to buy more, to buy at full price, to buy on impulse, and to avoid discounts. Stores are in the business of making money and Christmas is when they can make a killing.

Many stores make a large part, if not the largest part, of their profit during late November and December. For example, jewelry stores make almost a third of their sales during the holiday season, and department stores and clothing and apparel stores make about a quarter of their sales at this time.

PLAN FOR CHRISTMAS EXPENSES—CHRISTMAS IS NOT AN EMERGENCY!

While it might seem contrary to the spirit of Christmas, consumers should plan for this expense in the same way that they plan for taking a vacation or paying for fuel oil in the cold months. To not have a plan is to invite disaster, to be at the mercy of predatory retailers, and to be left with "credit card hangover" in January.

"Credit card hangover" means that after Christmas you are surprised by the amount of money that you charged for the holiday and also the increased payment(s) you'll have to make to pay it off. This probably happened because time was short and you began to charge a number of things without really paying attention to your total Christmas spending.

So what can you do about overspending without becoming a Scrooge? Simple. Plan ahead—Christmas is not an emergency.

Buy Gifts over the Entire Year

You will know, more or less from year to year, the people on your Christmas list and their individual likes and dislikes. Make a list, and all during the year, not just the holiday shopping season, buy presents when you come across appropriate gifts at a low price.

BE A SELF-AWARE SHOPPER

US News & World Report finds that each consumer should learn "How to Be a Self-Aware Shopper." This means that you learn to become aware of stores' manipulative environments. In addition, never buy when you feel anxious, guilty, or overexcited. Money, especially your money, is serious stuff. Buy only when you have a clear head. You should understand that stores have one goal: to get you to open your wallet and keep it open.

BEWARE CHRISTMAS MUSIC!

With so much money at stake, stores will pull out all the stops at Christmas, such as playing Christmas music and using nostalgia-inducing Christmas scents, to put consumers into a warm and fuzzy Christmas spirit, according to *US News & World Report*. The article went on to say, "Whether being stimulated by sound or smell, consumers are usually blissfully unaware of the fact that they are shopping under the influence." "The average consumer doesn't understand that they are being manipulated in that environment," says Anna Mattila, associate professor of marketing at Pennsylvania State University.

AVOID SHOPPING AROUND CHRISTMAS UNLESS ABSOLUTELY NECESSARY

During the holiday shopping season, you will find few if any sales, crowded stores, and lots of reasons to pull out your credit card and buy on impulse.

GET A FULL REFUND IF YOU TAKE CHRISTMAS PRESENTS BACK

When you get a refund don't forget to get the tax back and be aware of a couple of scams associated with refunds. Any money that stores can keep when you return a product adds to their profit. As a result many stores refund the price of the item but "forget" to refund the tax that was also paid. This is especially true if your receipt includes a number of items, therefore making the tax refund less obvious and harder to calculate. Also, many stores offer a "gift receipt" that has the item listed but not the price. Let's say you got a bathrobe under the Christmas tree but the day after Christmas you returned the robe to the store. As we all know, Christmas items often go on sale the day after Christmas so many employees will refund the sale price of the bathrobe but not the full price. Yet the full price is what was paid and what should be refunded. However, if you are working with a gift receipt you are flying blind, because you don't know the actual price the robe was bought for. If you are ever in this situation, you should insist on verifying the cost of the robe for the time when it was bought and getting a refund based on that. If full price was paid, you should get a full refund.

Appealed to a Higher Candy Corn Authority

*A*t the CVS pharmacy, in Greenlawn, New York, the eyes of Tanya Williams, a grandma with a gaggle of grandkids, widened when she saw a basket in the discount aisle filled with candy corn cut to 25 cents a bag after Halloween from a whopping $1. Williams told a young sales clerk she wanted to buy all the candy, but at a dime less than the sale price—15 cents a bag. He balked, but the manager she appealed to didn't. Appropriately, he was very sweet and she got it all at her price. "I've gotten good buys on Christmas candy, too," Williams said. We bet she did!

Summary: Money-Saving Tips for Holiday Time

- Plan for Christmas expenses so you don't overextend.
- Buy gifts over the entire year so you are not wiped out at Christmas.
- When shopping, be aware that you are in an environment that wants to separate you from your money.
- When you get a refund, don't forget to get the tax back.

Chapter 13

HOME IMPROVEMENT

*H*ome improvement complaints have been on the rise—up 60 percent over the last five years, according to the Council of Better Business Bureaus—so it certainly pays to take some steps to protect yourself, not just against contractors who would rip you off (a small minority) but also against contractors who simply don't know what they're doing, or have limited experiences. One consumer affairs commissioner in Massachusetts said that "some people get a pickup truck and a hammer and think they're a general contractor."

HIRE A RELIABLE CONTRACTOR AT A GOOD PRICE

START WITH A LIST OF GOOD CANDIDATES

Find names of contractors from friends who have used them successfully, or from building supply places—they know who the good contractors are and will not give you the name of someone who's not good since they don't want you coming back to them with blood on your hands. You can also get names from your local church, or a place like Angie's List (www.angieslist.com), where you pay $40 a year and get to read objective reports on particular contractors by people who have used them—in other words, ordinary consumers such as yourself.

Research the job thoroughly. Before you ask for bids—and you should get three—you could research the job and find out what products and materials you want to use. Note that one manufacturer may have ten or twenty-two product grades with the same brand name, as CertainTeed has for siding. You must know all details of the job, down to the model numbers of products.

Cut the Cost of Construction by 10 Percent

A small contractor told us this simple trick. When building a new home or a new shed, design it so that it takes standard-size lumber—savings are typically 10 percent. This means that the lumber won't need to be cut—which saves labor, material expenses, and the cost of hauling scrap materials away from the construction site.

GET THREE BIDS FOR A JOB

Generally, if you get three bids you'll get a high, low, and in between. The in-between bid is usually the way to go. You shouldn't automatically take the lowest offer when hiring a contractor. You should like his work, and feel you can get along with him. Make sure contractors bid for the same job, so you are comparing the same materials and specifications.

Check all possible contractors out at your consumer affairs department or state attorney general's office for licenses and any complaints. This is generally vital in many areas because if a contractor isn't licensed, the consumer affairs department won't get involved if you have a complaint. In many areas, too, states, counties, and cities have contractor restitution funds to pay you money if a contractor defaults on a job in some way (see the sidebar "Contractor Restitution Funds") but only if the contractor is licensed. Arrange your own financing for the job. Don't let the contractor do this for you. Additionally, ask the contractor for a list of twenty-five to fifty ex-customers and call a couple.

Price Warms Her Heart

*A*s reported in *Reader's Digest*, when Sally Greenberg, a Consumers Union attorney, needed a new furnace for her Washington, D.C., home, she went to www.checkbook.org. to find out which installers were rated best by consumers (as we said, www.angieslist.com is another site). She invited the top three to visit her basement and give her a written estimate. Their prices were $2,800, $3,100, and $3,800. She called the two with the lowest prices—she figured the costliest one probably wasn't going to budge enough to be competitive— and told the pair the job was between them. "Then I asked if they could come down in price." Both called the next day. Greenberg went with the lowest bid, $2,600, a savings of more than $1,000.

Sally Greenberg's experience is not unusual. It is possible, as mentioned in the introduction, to chop tens of thousands of dollars off home improvement jobs if you get bids. The best way to price a job is to follow what she did, but, of course, make sure that the contractors are bidding for the same job. In other words, the product quality and work to be done should be the exactly the same and spelled out in the contract and plans, if any.

BEWARE THE LIEN LAW

The lien law basically states that if a general contractor doesn't pay his independent subcontractors, or pay for his materials, you are responsible, even though you gave money to the contractor so he could pay them. Sounds insane, but that's the way the law is, and many a homeowner has been shocked when a sub, say an electrical contractor, shows up at the house and tells the homeowner that he's there to get his $4,000 for electrical work. When the homeowner protests that he or she paid the general contractor, the electrician responds, "But he didn't pay me." To free yourself from this scenario, you need a lien release. You might be able to get just one lien release from the general contractor if he or she regularly employs the people on the entire job such as plumbers, electricians, and carpenters. However, if the general contractor uses subcontractors, you will need to get a lien release from each of them.

Finally, and most important, control the money you pay the contractor. It's your only leverage. Hence, in most cases you shouldn't give an advance. If the contractor says he needs the money for supplies, ask him why he can't put it on credit. If he insists on an advance and you like him enough to pay something, offer 10 percent, which is what California authorities suggest (10 percent or no more than $1,000 on a $10,000 job and up).

You should arrange payments so that you pay only for completed work, something you can calculate by the number of days a job takes. If it's a five-day job, then you can pay 20 percent after 20 percent of the work is done, 40 percent after 40 percent of the work is done, and so forth. Money is the name of the control game.

Contractor Restitution Funds

*I*n recent years, so-called contractor restitution funds have increased. If such a fund is available, the county or state government will pay the homeowner out of a special fund if the contractor goes bankrupt or refuses to finish incomplete work or fix poor workmanship. Though the law varies from jurisdiction to jurisdiction, the contractor usually must have a home improvement license (one reason why it's crucial to hire a *licensed* contractor) and the consumer must get a judgment in court to get the money. Years ago, there were relatively few restitution funds, but this has changed, and the amounts consumers can get have also gone up. For example, Arizona residents can get a $30,000 refund; Alabama consumers, $20,000; Virginia residents, $20,000; Marylanders, $15,000; New York City residents, $15,000; Hawaiians, $12,500; Nassau County, Long Island residents, $10,000; and Suffolk County, Long Island residents, $5,000. Call your local consumer affairs department or attorney general to see how much you can get.

SIX MOST COMMON RIP-OFFS

There are a number of home improvement jobs where you have to be particularly vigilant. Following are the top six, in our view, and what you can do to protect yourself and save literally tens of thousands of dollars.

ASPHALT ROOF REPAIR/REPLACEMENT

One rip-off here is a contractor telling you that you need a new roof, at a cost of $5,000, because, he says, the leak inside the house you contacted him about is "coming through the shingles." The rip-off artist will confirm that and say, "Yes, that indicates you need a new roof." In fact, in 99 percent of the cases roof leaks occur because the sealing around vent pipes that project through the roof, or around the chimney or the flashing—the flexible metal that seals between roof sections—has failed. Replacing the sealer—simply and cheaply—solves the problem.

Of course you may need a new roof, but recognize the standard symptoms: curling shingles and missing shingles. Another telltale sign is loose granular material from the ceramic material that coats the tops of asphalt shingles. When shingles wear, these granules come off as rain and snow water wash down them into gutters. The sandlike granules build up in the gutters and indicate the shingles are failing. An asphalt shingle roof normally lasts fifteen to twenty years.

If you need a new roof, make sure you aren't talked into having the bad roof torn off—at a 50 percent increase in the cost of the job (unless it's so far gone it's necessary, or the town building code demands it). Many town buildings departments will allow a second, even a third roof to be installed if it is determined that the framing can support the weight. To prepare the old roof the roofer will cut off the curling portions and replace missing shingles to create a tight, solid base. If your roof is the thick "dimension"-style shingles, a "tear-off" must be done.

"The newest rip-off in roofing," says Northport, New York, roofing expert Ed Lindstadt, "is when you live in the U.S. where ice forms on the roof. The roofer doesn't tell you about the ice and snow membrane, because it will allow him to make a lower bid than competing contractors who do." This membrane is well worth the expense and can prevent costly roof damage since the material guarantees 100 percent protection against ice dams, which collect water that can then seep under the shingles and into the house. "But to install it," Lindstadt says, "the roof must be stripped to the deck—the wood base the roofing is nailed to—an extra cost, and the installed cost of the membrane is $70 to $100 per roll and would require three to five rolls to cover three feet up the edge of the roof."

Another roof rip-off is when the roofer tells you you need a new deck—for thousands of dollars. In fact, a whole new deck is needed only one in a thousand times. A small portion of the deck may need to be replaced because it's soaked with water, but this does not happen often.

CHIMNEY INSPECTION, CLEANING, AND REPAIR

The longtime favorite scam of the larcenous chimney sweep is the "bait and switch," and it is still very popular. You may see an ad for cheap chimney service, or someone will call you. Tom experienced the newest version of this one evening when someone called him and said the company was in the neighborhood and had just completed work on a neighbor's chimney. When Tom started to ask for details about this neighbor, they hung up.

Whatever the method, homeowners are enticed into having their chimneys inspected for some ludicrously low price, say $39.95. This price gets the scamsters in the door and into the chimney where that old standby, scare tactics, are then used to prompt homeowners into paying for a variety of expensive and unnecessary repairs, such as repairing nonexistent holes, or repointing mortar that is in good condition. In one sting conducted in Suffolk County, Long Island, seventeen of twenty-seven chimney companies estimated that work costing between $400 to $2,800 was needed on a chimney that was, in fact, in perfect condition, and two of the contractors said carbon monoxide levels were so high the inhabitants were advised to get out of the house immediately.

There is no question that fireplace chimneys can be hazardous. The smoke that rises through them results in the buildup on chimney walls of a blackish substance called creosote. If it gets to be more than a quarter inch thick, it may trigger a fire. For this reason, as well as to check the structural soundness of the chimney, experts recommend an annual inspection be conducted. This may cost $100 to $250 (not that ridiculous $39.95) and if cleaning is required, an additional $100 to $150. Fire departments in many communities will conduct the inspection, which, according to Mike Blake of the Durham, New Hampshire, fire department, takes about an hour, for free. Why free? They're trying to prevent a fire from occurring.

Chimneys for oil burners and gas burners are far less a concern than those that handle units where wood is burned. In fact, Kevin Rooney of the Oil Heat Institute of Long Island says that a properly maintained oil-heating system (serviced prior to the heating season) hardly ever causes problems.

Carbon monoxide poisoning from debris-blocked chimneys is also hawked as a severe threat, the danger often exaggerated, although having a carbon monoxide detector in the house is a good idea.

Because chimney sweeps have such a terrible reputation, one must make an extra effort to get one who's honest and competent, besides following the general tips for hiring contractors given earlier. If you can, hire someone with professional credentials. A so-called certified individual who has been taught and tested by the Chimney Safety Institute of America is good. There are some two thousand "Certified Chimney Sweeps" in the United States. Affiliation with these or similar organizations doesn't confer sainthood, but it is much better than nothing. Also, you should watch the technician as he makes his inspection. It is becoming common for sweeps to use video scanning equipment, where a tiny TV camera is fed down the flue to examine walls, etc. You should ask to see the resulting video and let him explain it to you as you watch it.

Finally, if your fire department doesn't inspect for free, ask if they can recommend a reliable pro.

BASEMENT WATERPROOFING

Like other rip-offs, ones involving keeping water out of the basement involve contractors using fear—just read some of those terrifying websites by waterproofing companies on the Internet—to trigger unnecessary work which can get quite expensive, into the thousands of dollars. The newest scams are from companies who present elaborate, art-filled websites that convince the uninitiated that the company knows what it is talking about.

The big idea in solving wet basement problems is to understand what is going on and to first try simple solutions before calling in professional help. The simple fact is that most basements can be protected against water intrusion quite simply—and cheaply.

"You should think," says waterproofing expert Rich Barako, "of your masonry foundation as a rigid sponge." If the water volume is above normal, it will become saturated and water will wick through into the basement. Of course if there are cracks it will get in even faster. Hence the big idea is to reduce the volume of water getting to the foundation. John Condon, a professional engineer at Condon Engineering, of Mattituck, New York, says that most of the time the water comes from clogged gutters that spill water onto the ground, improperly routed downspouts that route it there, and/or improperly sloped land around the house, which washes groundwater against the foundation. Improperly aimed lawn sprinklers can also cause problems.

Just clear the gutters and reroute the downspouts. Or use fresh soil and pack it five or six inches high against the foundation. Then gently slope it back to ground level. (People who live on hilly land can have dry wells installed to catch water so it's collected before it hits the foundation.) If water is still coming into the basement, repair any cracks with a product called hydraulic cement and then apply a top-quality waterproof paint such as Drylok, which, Barako says, works most of the time to stop the water. If this doesn't work, you can go to a mason-supply store and pick up a tarlike product that's used for waterproofing house foundations. Although it requires professional work, it can be applied to the exterior of the foundation following excavating the soil and cleaning the wall. This material dries to a rubbery consistency and will seal any cracks in the foundation, which are usually the cause of the leak. He estimates it costs about $1,000 for the average foundation wall.

Predators lurk in the basement repair business. To make sure you get an objective, competent, honest opinion, you might consider hiring a professional engineer or a home inspector affiliated with the American Society of Home Inspectors (ASHI). He or she can tell you how to solve the problem. ASHI members are continuously involved in increasing their know-how and are monitored for professionalism. Damp walls may also simply be caused by high humidity. To test, tape a piece of aluminum foil on the foundation wall; if moisture shows up on the patch in a day or two, you'll know it's condensation and you can start shopping for a dehumidifier.

Sometimes leaks on a floor indicate what is known as a "high water table." Rivers of water run under the house and during wet times their level rises and the water pushes through the concrete floor. In this case, one common solution is to have a sump pump installed. It collects the rising water and feeds it out of the basement through a tube.

TERMITES

If a technician is coming to your home, it's a good idea to arm yourself with a few facts about termites so you can ask questions that will lead to him showing you evidence of their presence. The most common type of termite is the subterranean. They live in columns in the earth near homes and burrow through it to get to their two staples, food (wood) and water. They are tiny—one-eighth of an inch long with a broad waist and longish wings. You are much more likely to have them if you live in a warm state than in a cold one. Most termites don't like cold. (Alaska has no termites.) To get to the wood in your house, termites construct mud tubes to travel up the foundation, and may also make pinhole marks in the base of the drywall as they forage for food. Mud tubes may be hidden behind siding. If termites are eating the wood, it will look hollowed out and clear of sawdust. Other insects or fungi leave completely different tracks.

Ask the termite technician for proof—mud tubes, pinholes, and/or damage—of their presence as suggested above. It usually does take a pro to find termites, but you may see signs of them yourself. In the spring they "swarm" inside the house, creating a cloud of bugs, part of their mating ritual. You may not see them swarming, but you could well see their wings, which they shed prior to mating.

Don't confuse termites with flying ants. Termites have a full waist rather than a pinched one, as ants do; wings that are the same length, rather than different lengths as ants have; and straight antennae rather than elbowed ones.

There are over seventeen thousand pest control firms in the

United States. Some are big and some are small but bigger doesn't necessarily mean better. You should base who you hire on good recommendations. You want someone who has lots of experience and will do the work for a fair price. Also, says Michael Potter, a professor of entomology at the University of Kentucky, ask the company to send one of its most experienced technicians. You don't want someone showing up who's been on the job a week or two. If he finds termites, ask him to lead you to the part of the house where they're located and show you.

You should get estimates from two or three companies. Some will charge many thousands of dollars for a job that should cost under $1,000. When they give their bids, take notes on the precise treatment they're going to do so you can compare properly. Treatment for termites may be "monitored baits"—traps set in the ground at intervals around your house—or "barrier" protection, where chemicals are poured or pumped into the ground. Which technique is better? That's up to the technician.

Don't Panic About Termites

It takes termites about five years to build a mature colony that can disperse and make new colonies and they eat slowly and not that much: A mature colony of 250,000 individuals, for example, consumes about one standard eight-foot two-by-four a year.

One rip-off is to use ineffective chemicals, or a new one on us, to use water. If you have any doubts about what went into the ground, you can contact your local Department of Agriculture and ask them to conduct a test.

Another rip-off is the too-short guarantee—say, a year. This is given because the scamster knows that after his treatment termites may come back—but after his guarantee has expired. You should sign up for nothing less than five years, and it should be a "repair guarantee," that is, the termite company is responsible for repairing damage the termites do. It will cost you about 10 percent of the original fee per year and is well worth it.

ASPHALT DRIVEWAY PAVING

It's a good idea for the homeowner to oversee, as much as possible, all aspects of building an asphalt driveway, because there are a number of things that must be done right to make sure the driveway works well and lasts for the many years it should.

The soil surface must be dug down to about seven inches and then rolled. After that a good herbicide must be sprayed on the ground to ensure that weeds can't grow through any gaps in the asphalt. The crushed stone base must be at least four inches deep, with three-quarter-inch pieces working well. The rip-offs come when the base that's laid is less than four inches or contains small stones that don't work well. Result: movement and a driveway that cracks. On top of the stone goes the hot-mix asphalt, which comes off the truck at about 300 degrees. It is installed in what is known in the trade as "lifts," one two-and-a-half-inch lift followed by another half-inch top. Each lift is steamrollered and together dressed down to about 3 inches. If the lifts are thinner you're being ripped off, since they will lead to the driveway cracking.

Be careful of an inferior mix. A scam-minded contractor will use asphalt labeled "commercial grade," which is a pastiche of materials that add up to poor quality. What you want on your driveway is the same quality hot mix used on highways. To get it, call the public works department in your area and ask for the "specs" on the asphalt they use and have your contractor write those specs into the contract, as well as the other stipulations mentioned above (four-inch base of three-quarter-inch stone and four inches of hot mix).

Also, although this is not a rip-off per se—it's more like incompetence—you should make sure that the driveway is pitched or crowned (raised in the middle like a spine) so water drains away properly and not into, say, the garage. It is a frequent mistake.

Beware the Williamsons

*I*f someone knocks on your door and suggests that he has some extra material—roofing, hot-mix asphalt (or anything for that matter) "left over from another job," and he'll give you a "good deal," you should do two things: say you're not interested and close the door. Door-to-door scams are quite common, and there are even groups—generally known as "The Travellers" or "The Williamsons"—who travel in new trucks and good uniforms and look quite legitimate. But they are not. They usually arrive in the middle of the day when only the woman of the house will be home so they can better intimidate her. Older people are also prime victims. And if you give them a chance, they'll not only rip you off on the repair job, but steal something when you're not looking.

MOLD "REMEDIATION"

When it comes to mold scams, fear is the key and the new tool for implementing it is the Internet. The ads make mold sound like the bubonic plague and hucksters make it sound like they have the last word on mold. One company even sells books that purport to explain the various kinds of mold. It's all designed to get you to authorize investigation and remediation. In fact, what you need to know about mold is simple: It is not dangerous to healthy people. If you have a problem with your immune system, says Dr. David Callahan of the Centers for Disease Control and Prevention (CDC), or have allergies, or asthma, it can be problematic. But it is not problematic for people without these health issues, other than the mold sometimes "smelling," he says.

Some scam artists will also want to run expensive tests to see what kind of mold is present, and then recommend a remediation company for removing the mold, a company they are in cahoots with. In fact, the CDC does not recommend testing, simply because no matter what kind of mold is present, if it's a problem to the occupants, it should be removed, and all mold is removed the same way. The CDC recommends that any area that is ten square feet or less be cleaned with soap and water followed by a solution made with a cup of bleach and a gallon of water. Both the CDC and EPA have plenty of good information on every aspect of mold on their websites (www.cdc.gov and www.epa.gov).

The key to clearing up mold, however, is eliminating excess moisture. As Pat Huelman, associate professor of the Department of Bio-feed Products at the University of Minnesota, says, "Moisture is the root cause of all mold problems." Steve Klossner, a Minnesota-based building expert, says that he has been in "lots of moldy houses, but has yet to find a house with a mold problem."

Summary: Money-Saving Tips for Home Improvement

HIRING A CONTRACTOR

- Get multiple bids.
- Make sure the contractor is licensed.
- Check references.
- Invite bids based on the same job, apples to apples.
- Most important: Control the money.

COMMON RIP-OFFS

Roofing

- You do not necessarily have to have all roofing stripped off (at a cost of 50 percent extra) when installing a new asphalt shingle roof.
- Only 1 in 1,000 "decks" need replacing.

Chimney Cleaning and Repair

- Hire only members of the Chimney Safety Institute of America.
- If a video is made of the interior of your chimney, watch it and have the contractor explain why it shows repairs or cleaning is needed.
- The chimney sweep field has a lot of rip-off artists in it.

Wet Basement

- 98 percent of the time the solutions are cheap and simple and involve keeping water from flowing against the foundation.

Termites

- Beware being overcharged.
- Understand how termites get into your house.

Asphalt Driveway

- Make sure the base and asphalt layers are thick enough.
- Check asphalt for quality.

Mold "Remediation"

- Mold is harmless to everyone except people with allergies or immune deficiencies.

Chapter 14

INSURANCE

$\sum$ ince you pay for insurance year in and year out, you can save a considerable amount by doing a bit of math, shopping around, and then raising your deductible while at the same time making sure that you have full coverage. The savings can be considerable, as you will be paying less year after year.

NOTE: See the automobile section for tips about saving on auto insurance.

BUYING INSURANCE

MAKE SURE YOUR HOME IS ADEQUATELY INSURED

Before shopping around for insurance, do some basic math. Your house should be covered not for its market value, that is, what it would sell for on the open market, but rather what it would cost to rebuild it if it were damaged (known as the replacement cost). Many insurance companies will only pay a reduced settlement if your home is damaged and not properly insured for the replacement cost. In addition, this coverage should probably go up every year.

Insurance Agents Lie

Some insurance agents tell homeowners that they have adequate insurance when, in fact, they do not. Without insurance that covers the replacement costs (that is the cost of replacing a house—not the market value of the house), many homeowners have to pay out of pocket for expenses they thought were covered by their policies. Insurance agents often "lowball" their clients because they do not want them to start shopping around and buying insurance from a competitor.

COMPARISON SHOP FOR INSURANCE RATES
- *Government information provides reliable, unbiased insurance cost comparisons.*

To find a price comparison for homeowner's insurance in your state, go to the Department of Insurance website for your state and look for "homeowner's insurance price comparisons." We've found that, in general, state websites offer extremely detailed price comparisons for homeowner's insurance for specific towns and regions. And cost, depending on the insurance company, can vary shockingly. For example, the Texas Department of Insurance shows a range of $420 to $1,231 for the same homeowner's coverage in Beaumont Place, Texas. This site also lists about five hundred towns in Texas, with rates for eight different kinds of homes from about thirty insurance companies along with a complaint index for each company. Now that's comparison shopping!

COVERAGES: Dwelling Coverage A: $100,000; Other Structures Coverage: $10,000; Contents Coverage: $300,000; Additional Living Expense Coverage: $10...
Personal Liability Coverage: $300,000; Medical Payments Coverage: $1,000; $500 Flat Deductible.

CHARACTERISTICS: A two story, single family dwelling with single-cylinder dead-bolt locks, one fire extinguisher, and two smoke detectors. Excellent condition, masonry or frame (composition roof), built in January, 2007.

* This insurer does not provide coverage for this hypothetical.

Premiums shown are annual premiums as of March 1, 2008.

| NAME OF INSURER | I PHOENIX | | II MESA | | III PEORIA | | IV FLAGSTAFF | | V TUCSON | | Complaint Ratio | |
| | MASONRY | FRAME | MASONRY | FRAME | MASONRY | FRAME | MASONRY | FRAME | MASONRY | FRAME | # of Complaints (C) divided / Exposures (E) X 1000 = Com | |
											C	E
United Services Automobile Assoc	$239	$241	$231	$233	$217	$219	$266	$268	$215	$216	1	56,819
Arizona Home IC	276	276	251	251	238	238	300	300	251	251	3	14,817
Safeco IC of America	277	277	257	257	220	220	217	217	209	209	1	16,441
Armed Forces Ins Exchange	301	311	255	264	214	221	306	317	214	221	0	1,999
Pharmacists Mutual IC	312	349	312	349	312	349	312	349	312	349	0	916
First Liberty Ins Corporation	321	317	232	232	255	253	283	280	237	237	0	9,669
Milbank IC	325	376	250	288	241	279	224	256	215	244	0	2,275
Balboa IC	360	364	291	293	238	242	248	252	223	226	3	14,284
Sentinel IC, Ltd	367	367	335	335	322	322	293	293	287	287	0	16,578
Badger Mutual IC	375	406	303	328	241	258	241	258	241	258	0	115
Fidelity National IC	379	379	316	316	315	315	282	282	264	264	7	24,309

Typical comparison of homeowners insurance policies by a state department of insurance.

GET THE HIGHEST POSSIBLE DEDUCTIBLE FOR HOMEOWNER'S INSURANCE

The Insurance Information Institute writes, "If you can afford to raise your deductible to $1,000, you may save as much as 25 percent" on homeowner's insurance. And the savings from this high deductible may more than cover the cost of additional coverage based on the replacement value.

COMPARISON SHOPPING FOR INSURANCE SAVES $2,820 A YEAR

As reported in *USA Today,* the Pivnick family saved $235 a month by shopping around for less expensive insurance for both their car and homeowner's policies. The new policies had the same coverage as the old ones. If they had raised the deductibles, they would have saved even more!

BUY LIFE INSURANCE NOW

According to Consumers Union, now is an excellent time for people to lower their life insurance premiums. Premiums have dropped dramatically. To do it, start by taking a physical and following your doctor's advice for getting in shape before applying for a new policy. You can get quotes at www.accuquote.com. *Consumer Reports* says that "a 40 year old man with a $1 million, 20 year term policy could save $50 a month by cutting his cholesterol 30 points, $65 a month if he dropped fifty pounds to reach normal weight, and $165 a month three years after he quit smoking."

MAKING A CLAIM

IF YOU ARE OFFERED A SETTLEMENT FOR A CLAIM
THAT IS TOO LOW, DON'T ACCEPT IT

If the insurance company for your car or home will not budge or is slow to respond on a claim, we recommend that you file a complaint as soon as possible with the state's insurance department. The office that handles these complaints is often a consumer services division. Some people might be afraid to do this, thinking that their insurance company might refuse to renew their insurance after the consumer has filed a complaint. But the state insurance department keeps track of all insurance complaints and most companies will not want to further aggravate a situation—especially since the state insurance department has the authority to prevent a company from operating within that state.

BE WARY OF FILING CLAIMS

Actually making a claim, even a small claim, on your policy can cause major problems. This has happened to so many homeowner policyholders, it even has a name. It's called "use it and lose it," as was reported on CNN. Doug Heller, a spokesman for the Foundation for Taxpayer & Consumer Rights, commented, "It has been a very strange development. Consumers are being threatened with non-renewal for filing legitimate claims."

The way to prevent this problem and to get adequate insurance is to buy insurance with a high deductible. The high deductible accomplishes two things: You get a lower-cost policy (a lot lower) and you file fewer claims because you pay any small expenses out of pocket.

So if you follow our guidelines, you may end up paying less for more comprehensive insurance (except for small out-of-pocket expenses not covered by the deductible) with a much lower chance that your policy will not be renewed.

Screwed by Coverage That Was Too Good

A friend of ours had a rock-solid homeowner's insurance policy that covered everything that could happen to her home. She paid on the policy for a decade. Then all of a sudden she had a couple of small claims in quick succession. Soon after, however, the insurance company refused to renew her policy. After that she had trouble finding another company to insure her. When she did find one, the cost went through the roof. What had she done wrong?

This friend made the classic insurance mistake. She bought too much coverage and paid too much money. While insurance companies will never tell you, they do not like you to file claims and every claim is a red flag. Therefore as a consumer, it is much cheaper and much smarter to use insurance for an occasional major insurance claim and avoid filing a number of small claims.

BEWARE LOWBALLING CLAIMS
- *Lowballing a claim means that you are not adequately compensated for damages to your home.*

Insurance adjusters often offer 30 to 60 percent less to settle a claim than the amount of money it would take to restore a home back to the condition it was before damage occurred.

For example, Allstate was given advice by a consultant when the company wanted to increase its profits: "When a policyholder files a claim, first make a low offer, McKinsey advised Allstate. If a client accepts the low amount, Allstate should treat the person with good hands, McKinsey said. If the customer protests or hires a lawyer, Allstate should fight back."

This tactic has worked so well that the property-casualty insurance industry, which covers homeowners and cars, recorded record profits of $73 billion in 2006, up 49 percent from two years before. Remember these facts when fighting a claim.

GET TO KNOW YOUR STATE GOVERNMENT DEPARTMENT OF INSURANCE

Your state department of insurance is an invaluable and unbiased resource. Typically this department can provide consumer guidelines for getting adequate insurance, specific comparisons of the premium costs for different insurers in the state, and a procedure you can use to file a complaint if you feel you have not been treated fairly. To avoid confusion you need to understand that the department handles many aspects of insurance, such as the regulation and registration of insurance companies. As a consumer you should go to the consumer services division, where you will find helpful consumer buying and complaint information.

HIDDEN INSURANCE BENEFITS

Most drivers do not read their auto insurance policies until after their car is damaged. That's a mistake because many times there are hidden benefits: They're covered for things they don't know about.

"Drivers spend a lot of money on auto insurance, but too often they wait until they need to make a claim after an accident or emergency and don't remember what their policy will cover," said Steve Cox, Better Business Bureau spokesperson. "After a widespread emergency such as a flood, when many people are making claims simultaneously, it's important for car owners to ask the representative handling their claim about their coverage and deductible, as well as any options that are included, so they get their money's worth."

According to the Insurance Information Institute, comprehensive coverage will reimburse drivers for loss due to damage caused by something other than "a collision with another car or object," such as fire, falling objects, catastrophic storms, vandalism, or contact with animals such as birds or deer. This includes flooding. "Although many states do not require that you purchase comprehensive coverage, if you have a car loan, your lender may have required you carry it until your loan is paid off," said Carolyn Gorman, vice president of the institute. "Comprehensive insurance is usually sold with a $100 to $300 deductible."

Many drivers also have coverage for a replacement rental car, although they may not realize it because this optional coverage was added at such a minimal expense, usually just a couple of dollars a month. This coverage provides immediate access to a replacement rental car until repairs are made to their damaged car or they are authorized by their insurance company to purchase a new car.

YOU DON'T NEED TO PAY OFF YOUR CAR
IF YOU HAVE "GAP" COVERAGE

Drivers whose cars are totaled may not have to continue making payments on the balance they owe on the car if their auto insurance includes "gap" coverage. This coverage pays the difference between the amount the insurer pays for the totaled car and the amount the insured owes on their lease or loan.

Without this coverage, drivers are responsible for paying the remainder of their lease or loan even when their car is totaled.

If your car is damaged, report it ASAP. If your car is not drivable, your agent or claims center may be able to save you time and money by having the car towed directly to the repair facility instead of to a temporary storage facility. In addition, arrangements may be made immediately to provide you with a replacement rental car.

Know what your deductible is and any other additional charges before authorizing work. Expect your insurance adjuster, claims representative, or repair facility appraiser to review the damage with you and explain the repair process, including the use of original (OEM), recycled, or nonoriginal auto parts. Before authorizing repairs, know what your deductible is, as well as any additional charges you will be expected to pay once repairs are complete. Ask about warranties on repairs. Ask whether your insurer has a repair facility referral program that offers a written limited or lifetime repair warranty backed both by the repairer and insurer for as long as you own your vehicle.

Summary: Money-Saving Tips for Insurance

- Make certain your home is adequately covered.
- Get the highest possible deductible to reduce premium size.
- Check state government website for price comparison information.
- Don't accept offer for a claim that is too low.
- Get to know your state department of insurance.
- Some insurance agents lie.
- Understand the benefits in your auto insurance policy now, not after an accident.
- If you have "gap" coverage you don't need to pay off your car loan after an accident.

Chapter 15

TELEPHONE

🛒

*T*here are so many options today when it comes to phone service, it can get very confusing. We recommend that you keep it simple and be very careful of teaser rates with lots of asterisks that hide the true cost of a service.

LONG-DISTANCE PHONE SERVICE

LOOK FOR FLAT-RATE LONG-DISTANCE SERVICE

When you are tired of the asterisks and the mice type and the rates that are supposed to be spelled out at the phone company's website but aren't, you might start to look for a company that prices its phone service with a flat rate. Imagine a long-distance phone service where a minute was a minute. Where there were no extra charges or even taxes—they were all included in the price. Well, believe it or not, these services really do exist.

Called prepaid long-distance services, they are a hybrid type of phone service in which you call an 800 number first and then dial the person you want to call. This service is offered by companies such as www.tel3advantage.com and www.onesuite.com (you can sign up at their websites). You might think of these prepaid long-distance services as phone cards on steroids, but without all the problems of phone cards. You have an account that you can access from your home phone with virtually no hassle since the service will recognize your phone number. But you can also call from any phone at a flat rate. You can review your account online and see all your charges and you can recharge the service anytime so that you keep the same account. There are also no long-term contracts, monthly fees, surcharges, or even taxes.

We suggest you try this service for a while and if you don't like it, stop using it (since you won't be locked into a contract). If you do like it, get rid of your long-distance company, but keep your ability to dial an 800 number. And then guess what? You will have entered a world where 3 cents a minute anytime, anywhere in the continental United States is actually 3 cents a minute.

NOTE: Although prepaid long distance works like a phone card, it is quite different. Phone card pricing can often be especially tricky (monthly fees, maintenance fees, minimum minutes charges, expiration of minutes) and there have been numerous complaints lodged with the Federal Communications Commission about poor service with these cards.

Misleading Long-Distance Ad

If we were to give prizes for misleading ads, this one from Embarq phone service would certainly be a candidate. On their website the company states, "Enjoy local calling and unlimited long distance for $44.95 per month. Call anywhere in the US any time you want, for as long as you want." But investigation reveals that, like most landline services we have seen, calling out of your local area but still calling close to home are exceptions (known as local long distance) and this will add extra expenses that lead us to one conclusion: This deal is not worth it. However, to be fair, it is typical of many phone company offers. Instead we recommend a prepaid flat-rate long-distance service as we discussed earlier in this chapter.

CHEAP CALLS TO FOREIGN COUNTRIES

> • *An 800 long-distance service may allow calls to foreign countries from any phone for 10 cents or less a minute.*

If you make a call from your regular phone or your cellphone to England or Ireland or Mexico or Canada, you might pay a hefty rate. However, many of the prepaid long-distance services, such as www.tel3advantage.com and www.onesuite.com, have low-cost international calling rates—some less than 10 cents a minute to more than two hundred countries.

You can even use these services with your cellphone to save a bundle. Just dial the 800 number and then the number to reach the party in the foreign country. You then will be charged a standard cellphone domestic rate plus the cost of the 800 service to a foreign country—which should be much less than a call from your cellphone directly to a foreign country.

However, if you call when you have free minutes on your cellphone, such as late at night, you might be able to reach your party in the foreign country during prime time. For example, there is usually an eight-hour difference between Los Angeles and London, depending on whether or not we're on daylight saving time. If you call after midnight or 1 AM (when you may have free cellphone calling) from L.A., you will be reaching London after 8 or 9 AM.

CELLPHONE COSTS

PREPAID CELLPHONES PAY OFF

That great low-cost cellphone deal you got has a way of ballooning into a huge bill each month. Text messages, overages, roaming—you name it, there are lots of extra charges and you don't really know until you get your bill. We think that for many people, there is a much better way to go. As with prepaid long-distance service, you can buy prepaid cellphone service. While this is a bit more expensive per minute than a contract service with a carrier, you can control the cost because you'll know exactly how many minutes you have in your account both before you make the call and after you finish. There are quite a few prepaid services these days and recharging your account is often quite simple. For example, the Trac-Fone that we have used for a number of years now rarely costs more than $100 a year, and the cost of minutes keeps declining. And the minutes roll over year after year so that unused minutes are never lost.

NEGOTIATE A BETTER CELLPHONE DEAL
- *At the end of your contract you can haggle for a better cellphone deal.*

Mark Donovan, a mobile phone analyst, notes that after luring you into their cellphone fold, companies will take quite a while to earn their money back in the first year because of the considerable money it takes to secure a customer. Hence when the average customer is at the end of his or her contract, he or she is in a great bargaining position. To use this power, Donovan says, check the websites of the major carriers for new enrollment deals. Then find retailers who handle a variety of providers and ask them if they're willing to cut a deal with you. If you'd rather stay with your current carrier, do stay, but for less. To achieve this, call your company and tell them that you see that another company is offering more minutes. Can they do better? If the person talking to you on the phone can't do better, ask to talk with their "retentions" department and tell them you're thinking of canceling and see what they say. Donovan says that its possible for the average person to save $360 a year.

Check Your Cellphone Bills

*E*very year, contact your wireless provider to make sure you're on the best plan. You can save hundreds by switching.

OTHER PHONE SERVICES

INTERNET PHONE SERVICE (VOIP)

Other services, such as Vonage and cable phone service, are popping up all of a sudden. These services use the Internet and are called VOIP (voice over Internet protocol). They sound like a good low-cost deal for local and long-distance calling, but there is a lot you are not being told.

It's 2 AM and your 911 call is not being answered. If you read the fine print, you'll see a phrase in your VOIP phone contract, such as that 911 calls are handled differently by this VOIP service. Translation: Your call may not go through and if you care about using 911 in case of an emergency, you'd better understand how it works. We suggest you ask your neighbors who have either Vonage or cable phone service how 911 works with their phone system. But the bad news does not end here. If you have a power outage, your VOIP phone may not work. And don't count on your cellphone, because cell towers might lose power as well. Rick has lived through more hurricanes than he would like to remember, but what always impressed him was that the standard phone (yes that old-fashioned land-line phone) always worked when nothing else did. During the last fifteen years, the power has gone out over ten times, often for over a week—but the phone never failed.

Summary: Money-Saving Tips for Telephone

- Look for flat-rate and virtual phone card long-distance services.
- Overseas calls can cost less than 10 cents a minute for many countries.
- Consider a prepaid cellphone service to keep costs in check.
- Negotiate a better cellphone deal at the end of your contract.

Chapter 16

TRAVEL

It's safe to say that today's travelers, with airlines and hotels clamoring for their business, are in good shape to get discounts on both. Following is a lineup of ideas that will put you on the highway to big savings.

AIRLINES

BOOK EARLY

Book at least fourteen days ahead of time. However, the best rates are often found three months or more before you leave.

BE FLEXIBLE

If you don't need to leave or arrive at a certain time, give yourself some wiggle room. The savings on some flights can be dramatic. For example, if you can leave after the morning rush, you might save some money.

LOOK AT MORE THAN ONE DEPARTURE AIRPORT OR DESTINATION AIRPORT

It can cost a lot less to fly out of or into some airports. For example, Rick found that it was much cheaper, faster, and more convenient to fly to the Newark airport when he wanted to go to New York City, than to fly to Kennedy Airport where most New York City–bound traffic went.

Check All the Airlines

$\mathcal{S}$ome low-cost airlines, like Southwest, may not be listed on websites such as Orbitz (www.orbitz.com) that compare the prices of most major airlines. You may have to go to the discount company's own site. In the last several years we have usually found the very best deals at Southwest and other such discount, no-frills carriers. Look online for a list of all the airlines that fly out of your local airport.

BOOK WHEN THE AIRLINE IS SLOW

People often forget that the travel business is very cyclical. Vacation hotels are usually busier on weekends and business hotels are busier on weekdays. Saturday can be a slow day for airlines. Use your travel haggling skills in the valleys of these travel times to get the best deals.

HOTELS

BOOK A HOTEL WHEN IT'S NOT BUSY

The hotel industry calls them "shoulder seasons," those couple of weeks before or after the big tourist seasons, which are often very good deals. During these times hotels will bargain with you and restaurants and attractions will be open. If you want to take a vacation and your schedule will allow it, shoulder seasons are a great time to travel—cheaper and less crowded.

What Is the Shoulder Season?

*E*very trade seems to have its own language and travel is not exception. In travel there is a high season when things are busy and a low season when things are slow. The in-between time is neither high nor low, so it is called the "shoulder season." May and September, the times just before and after the summer peak, are often shoulder seasons in many areas of the United States.

NEGOTIATE DIRECTLY WITH THE HOTEL ON PRICE

For a really great deal, spend a few pennies and call the location where you want to book your stay. We have found that calling the local hotel will give you a much better deal than booking it online or calling the central office with the 800 number. The reason is simple: You're going straight to the horse's mouth. The local employees will have the best understanding of how busy they are and how much they are charging.

So what do you do when you are talking with a person at the local desk? First ask for the price for a room with your specifications. Then after getting a price, haggle. That's right, bargain, since hotel rooms are one area where you should always ask for a lower price. If the clerk you are bargaining with seems reluctant, talk to the manager. According to *Consumer Reports*, "More than 70% of [CU] survey respondents who haggled say they won a rate reduction or room upgrade."

We have found that discounts of 30–40 percent (and up to 50 percent in the shoulder seasons) are not unusual, and these discounts are often much better than what you would get with a discount card such as an AARP card. Also, once you have locked in a low price, you can try one more haggle. Ask for a free upgrade to a bigger room or a free breakfast or a free late checkout. Again we have found that even after agreeing on a low price, we can still get one of these extras.

Use an 800 Number to Get a Local Hotel Number

The best use for the central 800 number is for getting the phone number for the local hotel where you want to book your stay!

USE A LOYALTY CARD

If you have one of the hotel's loyalty cards (a usually free "club"-type card that gives you extra discounts as a loyal customer), flashing it often helps get you a free upgrade.

PAY LESS FOR SEVEN NIGHTS RATHER THAN FIVE

More can cost less. If you know you are going to stay at a hotel for five days, go ahead and lock in a seven-day weekly rate, which often costs less than five days. Even if you do not stay the full seven days, it gives you the option, for example, of checking out late without a penalty and also the option of staying another day if you are having a great time. For example, a motel in Wilmington, North Carolina, charged $250 for a full seven-day week, about $50 less than the charge for staying five days based on the daily rate.

When You Get a Low Rate on a Hotel, You Save Even More

*M*any tourist destinations charge a hefty hotel tax in addition to the regular sales tax. This often comes to 15 percent or more. This means that if you haggle a low rate for a hotel room, you not only pay less for the room, you also pay less in taxes. For example, a $100 room with a 15 percent tax would be $115 per day, while a $60 room would be $69 per day or $6 less per day in taxes.

RESOLVE YOUR PROBLEMS QUICKLY WHEN TRAVELING AND GET SOMETHING FOR YOUR PROBLEMS—FAST

Anne and Greg Hancock went to a Tampa, Florida, hotel. It was sort of a working vacation for Greg, a horse trainer. While he and Anne were at the hotel, they failed to get a scheduled wake-up call, which led to a slapstick series of events where Anne tore her slacks while rushing to get dressed and they were late for their appointment. They complained to the hotel management and asked what it was going to do as recompense. And management did three things: They bought them a free dinner, referred Anne to a local dress shop, where she picked out a pair of slacks and was not charged, and finally the manager called the horse training facility where Greg had the appointment and told the facility that it was the hotel's fault that Greg was late.

Anne and Greg are frequent travelers, so they explained that when it comes to a hotel making a mistake they knew that a bird in the hand is worth two in the bush. They weren't about to depend on promises that the management would take care of it later. "Try to resolve it quickly, when you are there," Greg said, "because once you leave, many hotels and tourist attractions won't be accommodating. We recommend that you ask for an upgrade or a free meal or complimentary tickets or some such thing, which most places should be able to supply you with. Most motels or hotels don't like to give money back but at the same time most are willing to give you something free to solve a problem."

We couldn't agree more!

BEWARE THE COST OF HOTEL PHONE CALLS YOU MAKE

Like banks, hotels keep looking for ways to nickel-and-dime you to death. The use of hotel phones is one way. Before you arrive at a hotel ask about charges for phone use, such as: Is there a charge for local calls? For 800 calls? For calls within the hotel complex? Many travelers have been hit with high unexpected charges after making only one call. If you use an 800 long-distance service, as we recommend (see our phone chapter), you can make all your calls, both local and long distance, using your 800 service. Generally there will be a flat fee or no fee for calling 800 numbers.

RENTAL CARS

SIX TIPS FOR RENTING A CAR

1. Check out the big travel sites, like Orbitz.com, Expedia.com, and Travelocity.com, to see if they can beat the prices on one of the travel search engines such as Sidestep.com. Other places to compare prices are Priceline.com, Hotwire.com, CarRentalExpress.com, and BreezeNet.com. You can also check

out prices at local and independent dealers to see if you can get a better price than with the big companies.

2. Beware, if you asked for an economy car rather than a mid- or full-size one and you get the latter. Economy can cost you up to $50 less than other sizes.

3. One worker at Avis in Kennedy Airport says, "If you pick up a car at an airport you'll pay extra, because of high demand for pickup there [almost 90 percent of all cars are rented at airports] and airport fees also fatten up the cost." To cut costs, she says, you might want to rent the car at an off-airport location, say downtown. You should determine if what you'll save on the car rental is worth what you'll save in terms of any extra costs incurred.

4. Check to see if your own insurance will cover you while you have the rental car. Rental companies offer two kinds of insurance: collision damage, which covers you if the car is stolen or damaged, and personal liability insurance, which covers for injury to nonpassengers. Some rental agencies also offer personal injury coverage.

5. A number of credit cards offer free insurance when you use that card to charge car rental fees. Before signing up for rental-car insurance, check what kind of insurance credit cards will cover damage-wise. Be aware that many American Express cards and many Visa cards will cover damage to the vehicle but not personal liability, though your own insurance policy will usually cover the latter, and your health insurance will cover personal injury. When you check, you should be aware where the insurance is in effect in terms of mileage and geographic limits. You don't want to be thirty miles beyond the mileage restriction and have an accident that isn't covered. If you have unlimited mileage on the rental car, you shouldn't have a problem. The central point here is to check to see what you can cover without plunking down additional dollars.

6. Be alert to extra charges that can creep into the picture, such as a $5 fee for allowing someone else to drive the rental, returning the car late, changing the drop-off location, or not returning the car with a full tank of gas.

Free Rental-Car/Hotel-Room Upgrade

*I*f you have reserved a subcompact car and none are available, ask for a free upgrade to the next size car. You should never pay for such an upgrade if the company could not deliver as promised. The same holds true for a hotel room. If you asked for an ocean-view room (usually at a bit of a distance from the ocean) but they are now gone, insist on an ocean-front room (a room directly on the ocean) or a much bigger room, or a breakfast at no charge. When a company does not do what it agreed to do, you are in a strong position to insist on a free extra.

MORE TRAVEL TIPS

GO ON A "STAYCATION"

To save money, many families are deciding to stay home instead of taking a two-week vacation. But they still need time off. The solution: Take a staycation, a vacation close to home. This will help you avoid paying for a lot of gas, hotels, and restaurants three times a day. The very good news is that since you will be close to home, you will have time to research all the attractions that are within a day's comfortable drive. Many people live for years in an area without realizing that on some days a museum is free or that a local park has special events on Friday nights or that there are free gardens in full bloom during certain months. (See "Philbin: Guilty as Charged.")

We recommend that you make a folder and collect announcements, calendars, handouts, etc., as you go about your daily routine. And who knows, you may discover that your local area is much more interesting than you ever imagined.

Philbin: Guilty as Charged

"*I* don't know why people don't travel to local attractions," says Tom. "I'm guilty, too. I was born, raised, and got married in the Bronx and I didn't visit the magnificent Empire State Building—about forty minutes away by train—until I was twenty-five years old."

TRASH THOSE FREQUENT FLIER MILES!

How much is a frequent flier mile worth? It turns out, not much. We now know airlines can change their rules in the middle of the game and decide that the value of a mile is much less than they said it was and there is nothing that you can do. For example, in July 2008, airlines announced that they would now be charging for formerly free trips bought with frequent flier miles. These add-on charges were generally $25–$50 per trip.

While a recent rash of new charges was caused by the rise in the price of oil, it simply continued a trend that had started years earlier. According to *The New York Times* in July 2008, "Airlines have already been tweaking their loyalty programs in recent years, making miles harder to redeem, imposing shorter expiration periods and raising the number of miles required for certain awards." The problem with frequent flier miles (in fact with all such rebate-type programs) is that they promise a discount sometime in the future. But before you cash in your carefully saved bundle of flier miles, a company can make drastic changes in the value of your account. It's not like money in the bank. (Maybe that's not so secure these days, either!) So what's an air traveler to do? Simple. Forget about frequent flier miles. We believe that you will do much better if you look for the lowest-cost fare and stop trying to book a more expensive flight that will give you bonus miles.

Summary: Money-Saving Tips for Travel

- Book early.
- Be flexible.
- Consider various departure and destination airports.
- Check all airlines for prices.
- Book when airline is slow.
- Book hotel when it's not busy.
- Negotiate directly when it's not busy.
- Use 800 number to get hotel number.
- Use loyalty card.
- Pay for seven rather than five days.
- Get payback for problems quickly.
- Beware cost of hotel phone calls.
- Get free car-rental/hotel-room upgrade if your reservation is not honored.
- Reduce your car rental costs.
- Go on a "staycation"—stay home and visit local attractions.
- Frequent flier miles are not worth much.

Chapter 17

MISCELLANEOUS EXPENSES, A TO Z

APPLIANCES

KNOW RESALE PRICE WHEN BUYING MAJOR APPLIANCES

The so-called resale price is an important price to know when you're buying an appliance. It is the price below which a manufacturer tries to not allow his product to be sold. The "list price," or shown price—the one you see attached to the appliance—is usually considerably higher than the resale one. So, when negotiating a price for an appliance, say to the salesperson that you'd like to purchase the appliance at the resale price, or ask to see the resale book. When you do this you are delivering a message: "I'm a knowledgeable shopper and I want the best price you can offer."

BATTERIES

BUY FRESH BATTERIES

Make certain the batteries you buy are fresh. Going to a store with large turnover can help here. Or ask the seller (manufacturers may stamp a date code on battery that the store—but not you—will know) for the freshest ones he has. The older the battery, the less power it will have. Also, don't store batteries near heat. This drains energy away, too.

BOATS

HAVE YOUR BOAT WINTERIZED AND
TUNED UP TOGETHER IN THE FALL

"Most people," says one boat dealer, "will get their boats winterized in the fall and tuned up in the spring. But it's a lot cheaper to have them both done at the same time in the fall because dealers need the business. In fact you'll be able to get both done for what a tune-up could cost in the spring."

BURGLAR ALARMS

BURGLAR ALARM PROTECTION NOT AS ADVERTISED

There is appearance, and there is reality. The appearance (on a TV ad) when it comes to home alarms is that a shifty-eyed burglar, dressed in dark clothing complete with skull cap and working on a window or door, suddenly breaches the alarm system, which results in alarms blaring, the perp fleeing, and a frightened resident getting a call from a neatly dressed, concerned individual at the alarm company reassuring them that help is on the way. And more or less by the time the resident hangs up, the police, bubble lights on their vehicle flashing, are pulling into the driveway. Your alarm, which has locked you into an expensive multiyear contract, has kept you and your family and your property safe.

The reality of home alarms is quite different. Today police are taking longer and longer to respond to alarms, up to a half hour and more. The problem is that many are jaded, and have developed a "cry wolf" mind-set. All over the country, most of the alarms that come in are false, because of mechanical flaws with the alarm system (or it being overly sensitive), a pet triggering the alarm, or, one of the worst culprits of all, an electrical storm. Typical is the town of New Castle, New York, where Police Chief Steve Fuchila says that of the roughly 160 calls they get a month and respond to, 99 percent are false. Many police departments have become so overwhelmed they have started fining homeowners and businesses. For example, the town of Kannapolis, North Carolina, recorded 99.3 percent false alarms. As a result the Kannapolis city government may start to impose fees that range from $50 after the first couple of false alarms to $500 for repeat offenders. Said one homeowner, "Five hundred dollars? Ridiculous. I'd rather be robbed."

Meanwhile, home protection is not cheap. A typical ADT system will cost $800 to $1,200, with a required two- to three-year contract plus installation costs. Happily, home protection can be achieved cheaply and without the worry or annoyance of false alarms. Many police departments will provide experts to come to your home and offer free advice about low-cost ways to protect it and yourself. Or the homeowner can download a number of checklists off the Internet from police departments.

One way we especially like to make a burglar think protection is being provided by a hi-tech system is to get some inexpensive stick-on labels to put on your windows. These labels state that your home is protected by a state-of-the-art alarm. Of course the experienced burglar knows that some of these stickers are false. But why, he also figures, take a chance? He most likely will move on to easier pickings.

CESSPOOLS

PRECAST CESSPOOLS BEST

As with so many other products, getting a cesspool installed can vary greatly in price, so you should absolutely shop around and haggle. Installers overwhelmingly advise getting a precast concrete pool rather than individual masonry blocks, though the former is a little more expensive. Says one installer, "You don't have to worry about it collapsing—block pools collapse after a certain number of years. Indeed, every time it's pumped, the walls are weakened because it's water pressure that holds the walls up. A precast pool will never collapse." Installers recommend that you get a three-section pool instead of just a two-section. It only costs a little more and gives you much more capacity.

Make Sure You Have Room for Installation

To install a precast cesspool you need property that's big enough to allow access for a crane, which is used to install the sections.

THE BIGGER THE PUMPING TRUCK, THE MORE IT MAY COST

If you're going to have your pool pumped of the "honey"—the trade term for sewage—the more capacity the truck has, the more you will pay. Explains one pro:

At the sewage disposal plant, they charge operators for the total gallonage of their trucks, no matter how many gallons in the truck. So if a man goes in to dump a 1,500-gallon truck, he will be charged, say $30—2 cents a gallon—even though he may only have 1,000 gallons in the truck. If someone has a 2,000-gallon truck, he will have to pay $40, even though he also only has 1,000 gallons in the truck. And the price goes up proportionately for the homeowner: "A man with a 1,500-gallon truck might charge you $90 and someone with a 2,000-

gallon truck $120." Hence you'll probably get a better price if you get someone with a smaller truck.

MAKE SURE THE POOL IS COMPLETELY PUMPED

When you get your cesspool pumped, make sure it is completely pumped. A rip-off is possible. Says one insider: "An operator will come to one house with a 2,000-gallon truck, and pump out the cesspool entirely, say 1,300 gallons' worth. Then he'll go to another house and will pump out whatever will fill his truck, and that's it. Then he only has to make one trip to the plant, but there might be 400 or 500 gallons of sewage still left in the pool."

You should either (a) ask the operator if his truck is empty enough to completely empty your pool, or (b) observe the pool being emptied.

COLLEGE COSTS

GET QUALITY BUT REASONABLY PRICED HIGHER EDUCATION

Some parents think they earn too much money to apply for financial aid, but this is not necessarily true, and parents should apply even if they think they won't qualify. To increase one's chances, it's a good idea to reduce one's cash flow before applying. To learn some strategies, click on www.finaid.org to pick up tips on how to do this, such as paying off auto loans and credit card bills. Be aware, of course, of other aid and scholarships, such as www.fastweb.com, www.college.com, www.Fafsa.ed.gov, and www.studentaid.ed.gov, and have a conversation with your child's guidance counselor about the best way to proceed.

If you are able to get some aid for your child, you may be

able to fatten it up if you've suffered in some way fiscally, such as losing your job or your spouse (and his or her income) since getting aid. Just call the college's financial aid office and explain the situation. Also, colleges, like retail stores, will match an aid package offered by another school, or even beat it if they want to bolster their student enrollment. It doesn't hurt to ask, particularly if the second college would have cheaper commuting or other costs.

You can also get need-based loans from colleges, such as federally subsidized Perkins loans for needy students who want to further their postsecondary education. You can read about these at http://www.ed.gov/programs/fpl/index.html. There are also non-need-based government PLUS loans that parents can take out to help their children. You can read more about these at http://studentaid.ed.gov/PORTALSWebApp/students/english/parentloans.jsp.

Free College? Yes!

It's hard to believe, but here's what Berea College says (and it's true) in its catalog: "Berea College is distinctive among institutions of higher learning. Founded in 1855 as the first interracial and coeducational college in the South, Berea charges no tuition and admits only academically promising students, primarily from Appalachia, who have limited economic resources."

Don't Forget About State and Community Colleges

*W*hile there are no definitive data available on how good state and community colleges are, one thing is for sure: They're a lot cheaper than regular colleges. "And they're just as good," avers Joe Beck, an English teacher in Bethpage, Long Island. "Learning is all about the professor," Beck says, "and there are good and bad ones everywhere. Also," Beck, who went to a state college, says, "you don't learn how to do your job until you're in the job." And a random survey had many more people expressing their support for state and community colleges than being critical of them.

COSMETICS

DON'T BUY THE BALONEY ABOUT COSMETICS

- *Low-cost and store-brand cosmetics are often as good as or better than brand-name products.*

Just because a cosmetic has clever gold packaging or a fancy name you can't pronounce doesn't mean it's better. Some products even have ego-stroking lines, such as "Because You're Worth It," attached to them to imply that if you use the product "you're worth it," and not worth it if you don't. This type of baloney is served up to make you buy the product, of course, and forget how expensive it is. Indeed, consumer expert Janice Lieberman says that cosmetics may be marked up sixfold. But Janice also writes that women can save a ton on cosmetics by shopping a bit more carefully, and avoiding ones with foreign-sounding names and expensive ones that are used as status symbols. If quality and stick-to-it-iveness is what you're after, the lower-priced items are often better. For example, Lieberman conducted a test and found that the cheapest lipsticks stayed on much better, and found that buying cosmetics from drugstores often costs "less than half of department store prices." Dr. Brad Jacobs of Beth Israel Medical Center in New York told her that "the only difference between expensive creams and cheaper ones" was "the packaging and fragrance." Therefore a $5 generic cream is often just as good as a $50 one (with a fancy name, of course). The best way to find out, Lieberman said, is to buy a small quantity of each cream. Bottom line: Go to your local drugstore and try the least expensive products first. Look in the mirror and trust your own skin and your own look.

KEYSTONING COMMON AT DEPARTMENT STORES

Keystoning means that products are marked up double rather than the usual 40 percent. Many of the better department stores "keystone" their prices.

FUNERALS
DON'T TRUST FUNERAL DIRECTORS

There is a classic story in *The American Way of Death* by Jessica Mitford about a woman who goes to buy a casket for her father. She doesn't have much money, and after looking around at expensive caskets that the funeral director shows her, she doesn't know quite what to do.

Finally, the funeral director says to her that he has one casket that may serve her well. She looks at it and it doesn't look bad. It's not superelegant, but neither is it like some of the terrible ones the funeral director has previously shown her. She tells the funeral director exuberantly that she will go for it. Fine, he says, but one question: "How tall is your father?" The woman says six feet. "Oh," he says, "in that case we'll have to take his legs off at the knees so he can fit in." Aghast, the woman agrees to go for a higher-priced casket.

The point of all this: Don't trust funeral directors. Some are fine, but some are not, and having a jaded philosophy is better than a trusting one. That being said, the following are some inside buying tips from an honest funeral director who, quite naturally, prefers to remain anonymous.

CASKETS AND BURIAL VAULTS

"If you're middle-class," he says, "don't spend a lot of money on a casket. It doesn't really pay to buy fiberglass or some other costly material, because the plain but gruesome fact is that the body rots from the inside out." The best buy for the average person, he says, is "a sheet metal casket with a spray metallic finish."

And what is a "burial vault"? This is trade lingo for the concrete box that the casket is set into and which is designed to keep the pressure of earth from crushing the casket. "The funeral director may well try to sell you one for $300 to $400 but a $150 box will do the job," one insider says. "A concrete box is a concrete box."

DON'T MAKE ANY BUYING DECISIONS WHEN YOU'RE GRIEF-STRICKEN

If a loved one has just died, chances are your judgment may not be at its keenest, so it's best to wait at least overnight. And you can do that easily. If your loved one dies at home, call the funeral director and ask him to take the remains to the funeral home, and the next day, when you're a little more settled, start talking "arrangements" with him. Funeral directors don't do this for free, so ask about the cost.

A Dignified Funeral for $800?

According to a consumer authority, "a loved one can be laid to rest with dignity for less than $800, by choosing cremation and using creativity." For example, comparison shop for funeral expenses since costs vary widely. Use an inexpensive heavy cardboard box for cremation, which is legal in all states when cremation is involved. One writer for the industry says, "Some funeral directors will try to sell you a $2,000 casket for a cremation, which is crazy because it's going to be burned up. So go with the least expensive casket."

EXTRA TIME AT HOSPITAL

If your loved ones dies in a hospital, then you could have the remains stay at the hospital, if you need the time, even for weeks, for an inconsequential charge. One other idea: Have a close friend make the arrangements. He or she is bound to be calmer than you.

DON'T LET THE FUNERAL DIRECTOR KNOW HOW MUCH YOU HAVE TO SPEND

As another insider says, "This is like telling any type of salesman what you can spend." Remember, beneath that kindly face and behind those sympathetic eyes is a businessman who wants to maximize his profit.

HAIRCUTS

DO-IT-YOURSELF HAIRCUTS

Haircuts can cost $180 a year (per person per household), but there is a simple cheap alternative, a device called a Flowbee (www.flowbee.com), which attaches to a vacuum cleaner and does a very good job of home hair cutting. Rick has been cutting his hair with a Flowbee for fifteen years. Doing twelve haircuts a year, he figures he's saved $2,700 (at $15 a cut) during that time.

The way it works is simple. A set of electric scissors runs while suction from the vacuum cleaner pulls hair into the cutters. Various spacers, up to six inches, are then used to cut the hair to the precise length that the user wants. The real advantage to this system is that it cuts with a layered look and if done properly (the company has a video) you can look as if the best hair stylist cut it. This system works best for people with fine to medium-thick hair who want a cut six inches or less.

JEWELRY

JEWELRY "KEYSTONED"

The average commercial jeweler will "keystone" his price, making the list price double what he pays—a 100 percent markup. So if you buy a $2,000 ring, his profit will be $1,000 if you pay list.

BEWARE JEWELRY IN CATALOGS

You'll pay even more if you buy jewelry displayed in those beautiful four-color catalogs in the jewelry store. These prices are "double keystoned," in other words marked up four times, because the company that sells to the jeweler wants to leave enough markup room for any and all jewelers, no matter how piggish. "So, for example," says longtime jeweler Art Hughes of Salem, Massachusetts, "you walk into a jewelry store, see an item in a catalog for $300, and the dealer says, when you ask for a discount, we'll give you $150 off on this $300 item. So he sells the item for that, but it only cost the store $75. He made a 100 percent profit."

YOU'LL PAY MORE FOR DIAMONDS THAN THEY'RE WORTH

One company in Africa, De Beers, controls 98 percent of all the diamonds in the world, and they put them out at the price they wish. "Actually," says one source, "a diamond is quite a common stone. They mine it by the millions of carats each year. There are many other gems that Mother Nature produced in much rarer quantities. Opal is one example. Another is topaz—not what most jewelers call topaz, which is quartz, but real, precious topaz. That stone can be purchased today for around $150 a carat and is mined in smaller quantities than thousands-of-dollars-per-carat diamonds. But a big selling job has been done on diamonds."

BEWARE BUYING JEWELRY AT MASS MERCHANDISERS

There are a number of outfits that sell supposedly discounted jewelry, and on any given day you can see lines four deep of people who think they're getting a bargain. "Actually," says our source, "what they're buying is inferior-quality merchandise. Low-quality stones in lightweight gold settings. We're constantly repairing the settings because they're so light that they twist and the stones pop out."

Sparkling Discount

"*I* had heard that you can get big discounts on jewelry items," said Lou Adler, a New York City salesman. "So when I went into Tiffany's in Manhattan for an engagement ring for my fiancée, I negotiated the price of a ring that was listed at $5,500 for $3,125!"

LUGGAGE

SMALL STORES BETTER FOR DISCOUNTS

The worst place to shop for luggage is usually a big department store. They carry big-name brands that require them to limit discounts to sale times. At small luggage shops, however, you can often get a better price. There is generally a 40 percent markup on luggage, and an insider says that you can get 20 to 25 percent off by negotiating the price.

BUY DAMAGED LUGGAGE

Luggage that travels the airlines often gets damaged, and the airline is required to replace it. So what happens to the damaged luggage? "It gets repaired," says one shop owner, "and then is resold at great discounts." For example, Tom was shown a $50 piece of luggage that had been "undented" and was now selling for $12.50. The dented spot was neatly covered by a travel sticker depicting the joys of traveling to Italy. Not every shop repairs luggage. It might help to ask the airline what shops they send damaged luggage to.

Beware Going-out-of-Business Sales

*S*ome stores specialize in going-out-of-business sales. They import a lot of junk and plaster the windows with signs. This won't usually snare the native of the city, but it does get tourists. One retailer says that he knows of a store on Fifth Avenue in New York that has "been going out of business for six and a half years."

MATTRESSES

EIGHT COST-CUTTING TIPS WHEN BUYING A MATTRESS

When shopping for a mattress, don't get hornswaggled into believing myths about them. Insiders in the mattress trade dispel the following supposed truths.

1. "All mattresses are the same." False. Different bodies desire different things. Best bet, says one sales associate: "Take your shoes off and spend fifteen minutes lying on the mattress at the store. It can predict whether you'll be comfortable over the long haul."

2. "Mattresses can't be discounted." "That's baloney," says one salesman. "If you don't get a healthy discount on a mattress or a freebie, you've been ripped off."

3. "To be good, a mattresses has to have high coil count." Not true. Experts say that a mattress with 390 coils should be fine because they tend be overdesigned.

4. "The more expensive a mattress is, the better it is." Simply not true. Period.

5. "When you move around in your sleep, it's because you're uncomfortable." Moving in one's sleep is normal. You may have a problem if the turning continuously wakes you up.

6. "You have to buy a box spring to keep the warranty in force." This line should include the word "sometimes." Not all warranties require a box spring. Check with the company you're dealing with. It's very possible the one you have at home is good enough.

7. "We have no interest in selling a mattress other than making a sale," said one salesman. Not true. Salesmen get "spiffs," from the abbreviation for "sales person incentive funds," which are commissions. The more expensive the mattress, the heftier the spiff. *Consumer Reports* says that "commissions can amount to about $100 a bed."

8. "A bed is more comfortable when lined with wool, cashmere, and silk." Again, baloney. Small amounts of these materials are used, and when other linings are placed on the bed, you can't feel those special materials.

MOVING

SIX TIPS FOR MAKING A CHEAPER MOVE

1. Tip the workers at the start of the day. "They'll work harder for you," says one.

2. Get at least three bids on a move. Bids can vary greatly.

3. Hire a brand-name mover like United unless you've gotten a specific recommendation on a brand X mover. If something is broken, you'll have an easier time collecting on the insurance.

4. Don't move on a weekend. Moving on Saturday or Sunday is usually more expensive because the mover will charge extra for the amount of weight that is loaded and unloaded.

5. Move during the first three months of the year. This is the slowest time for movers and you can haggle a better deal.

6. Check your homeowner's insurance to see if it covers the move. "Most homeowners don't know they have this," said one insurance expert, "but many policies include this benefit."

PIANOS

GUARANTEES NOT WORTH MUCH

Be aware that buying a piano with a guarantee doesn't usually guarantee anything. Explains a retailer: "A ten-year guarantee may sound great, but in practice it may not work out. For example if you have a cracked sounding board on a two-year-old piano, the company may be required to replace it under the guarantee, but you'll have to ship it to them—and pay the shipping costs." So if you live in New York and the manufacturer is in Iowa, you're dead in the water. A few companies, however, understand this and will pay for a repairman to come to your house. But there's another problem. Says the retailer, "Once repaired, a piano is never really the same again."

CUTTING A PIANO PRICE

A former piano retailer says that the price should be haggled over. Of course, as with anything else you're going to haggle over, you should have a sense of what the markup is. "It's usually about 50 percent," the retailer says, "though some retailers will mark it even higher than that in anticipation of it being negotiated down."

SHOULD YOU TRADE IN YOUR OLD PIANO?

If you are buying a new piano, you can trade in the old one, just as you would a car to get a reduced price. However, if you do this, it's unlikely that you can haggle a discount as suggested above, so it might be better to haggle a discount and sell your old piano privately.

BEFORE BUYING A PIANO, GET IT APPRAISED

Hiring a piano tuner to evaluate a used piano you plan to buy is a good idea unless you're knowledgeable about pianos. One dealer says, "The average person doesn't really know what to look for. And there are lots of rip-off artists on the market. If you're buying a new piano there usually isn't a problem if you stick with brand names, but an evaluation is still in order." The dealer explains that "pianos dry out, and this of course will affect function."

PRINTER COSTS

PRINTER CARTRIDGES

Ever wonder why computer printers are so cheap? Says one sales associate in Best Buy who, for obvious reasons, prefers to stay anonymous, "That's not how they make their money. It's the obscene price of printer cartridges." One way to save on cartridges is to get them refilled. Walgreens, for example, charges $10 to refill a black ink-jet cartridge and $15 for a color one. New cartridges normally cost over $60. Stores such as Quill and Cartridge World sell refurbished laser cartridges for laser printers at a good discount. For example Cartridge World sells a refurbished cartridge for an HP 1020 Laser Jet that is usually around $73 for $51—a 30 percent discount.

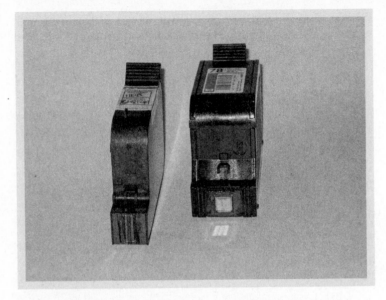

Instead of buying separate cartridges for an ink-jet printer at $60 or so, you can have them refilled at various places, such as Walgreens drugstore for $25 . . . a $35 saving.

RESTAURANTS

SENIORS CAN SAVE 10 PERCENT AT MANY FAST-FOOD JOINTS

Rick has been eating at Wendy's for more than thirty years. He frequents the local Wendy's so much, they know him by name. But they never told him about the senior discount that could have saved him 10 percent!

At another Wendy's in another town, an older employee looked at him and asked if he qualified for the senior discount. Since he was over sixty, he qualified. "I eat at Wendy's all the time," he said to her. "No one ever told me about this." She just shook her head. Now he always asks at Wendy's and they always give it to him, but he has to remind them every time, or he doesn't get it. And by the way, at Wendy's "senior" means fifty and older. Lesson: If you are over fifty, always ask about senior discounts and don't be embarrassed—it's your money you will be saving.

In the past, the following companies have offered senior discounts, have discounted senior menus, or have special offers for seniors: Applebee's, Krispy Kreme, the Waffle House, Arby's, Wendy's, Boston Market, International House of Pancakes, and Shoney's. In addition these companies offer free drinks or discounted drinks to seniors: McDonald's, Shoney's, Taco Bell, Hardee's.

Senior Discounts Are Everywhere

*I*f you are fifty or older ask at just about every store or business for a senior discount. We have found them at department stores (on Wednesdays), at the movies, at drugstores, at small local restaurants—you name it. It never hurts to ask.

WANT A SMALLER PORTION? ORDER OFF THE KIDS' MENU

A little-known way to save money and your waistline is to order off the smaller-portioned children's menu. My wife does this all the time at the Outback, for example. Now, she is not a kid, believe me, but not one single waiter in two years has objected or told her than she couldn't order from the children's section.

This seems to be one of those well-kept secrets in the restaurant business. Some restaurants might be harder to work with than the Outback, but remember, in this economy, with restaurants being affected more than most businesses, many will assume that the customer is always right.

WANT A RESTAURANT DISCOUNT? BE A TOURIST IN YOUR HOMETOWN

Just about every city of any size has a visitor's bureau or tourist center. While most local residents don't often think about it, you may be able to go to these offices and pick up coupons for a variety of restaurants and other attractions.

So put on your straw hat, strap a camera around your neck, and take a stroll over to your local tourist center. Then grab a bunch of coupons that the rest of your friends and neighbors don't know exist.

ALWAYS GET A DISCOUNT ON PIZZA

Many pizza restaurants (and other restaurants as well) put coupons in the yellow pages of the phone book. And you can find these phone books just about anywhere—at your work, in a phone booth, or at a friend's house. And most of these coupons go unused. However, with the owner's permission, you can carefully clip out a coupon from the phone book just about any time during the year—and then cash it in when you pick up your hot pizza.

Summary: Money-Saving Tips for Miscellaneous Costs

APPLIANCES

- Know resale price when buying a major appliance.

BATTERIES

- Suit batteries to use.
- Get fresh batteries.

BOATS

- Have your boat tuned up and winterized together in the fall.

BURGLAR ALARMS

- Ones you buy don't always work like they're supposed to.
- Simple, cheap tricks can make your house seem like it's very well protected.

CESSPOOLS

- Precast cesspools are best.
- The bigger the pumping truck, the more it will likely cost to pump a cesspool.
- Make sure your cesspool is completely pumped.

COSMETICS

- Don't believe what you read about cosmetics.
- Department stores "keystone"—double their prices.
- Some stores stay alive with phony "going out of business" sales.

FUNERALS

- Don't trust funeral directors.
- Don't spend a lot of money on a casket.
- Don't make any buying decisions when you're grief-stricken.
- If you need extra time, the deceased may stay free at the hospital they died at.
- Don't let the funeral director know how much you have to spend.
- Consider cremation.

HAIRCUTS

- Using a Flowbee, you can cut your own hair.

JEWELRY

- Jewelry keystoning doubles price.
- Beware jewelry in catalogs.
- You'll pay more for diamonds than they're worth.
- Beware buying jewelry at mass merchandisers.

LUGGAGE

- Small stores better for discounts.
- Buy damaged luggage.

MOVING

- Tip the workers at the start of the day.
- Get three bids on a move.
- Don't move on a weekend.
- Move during the first three months of the year.
- Check homeowner's insurance to see if it covers the move.

PIANOS

- Guarantees are not worth much.
- Haggle.
- Trade in old piano—maybe.
- Get piano appraised before buying.

RESTAURANTS

- Check for senior discounts.
- Order off the kids' menu for a smaller portion.
- Get tourist coupons.
- Find coupons for pizza in the yellow pages.

Chapter 18

XTRA—GET IT FREE

We are so used to paying for things that we often find it hard to believe that free stuff can be better than stuff you pay for. Yet once you overcome that prejudice, you will often find a slew of freebies that are as good as or better than what you can buy.

CALENDARS, ETC.

Businesses like to give a away calendars for the coming year because customers are reminded day after day about the business that gave them the calendar. At the end of the year Rick has found free wall calendars, desk calendars, record-keeping books, planners, and even small calendars that will fit in a wallet. He found these at hardware stores, banks, tax services, hardware stores, utility companies, and even from home repair companies. Some of Rick's favorites have been much better than he could have bought commercially, calendars such as one on bamboo from a Chinese restaurant or another from a hardware company with phases of the moon and *Farmer's Almanac*–type information.

SOFTWARE

For the IBM standard, at least, there is a ton of quality software available. Rick runs the equivalent of hundreds if not thousands of dollars of free stuff on his computer that is better than fancy-sounding paid software. Totally free software is known as "freeware" and there are no strings attached; nothing to buy, no spammy emails, no spyware. Why would a software developer simply give away free software? It turns out that there are quite a few reasons. Software is labor intensive but, if a software designer has the time, it can cost almost nothing to create. And putting out quality free software can give a computer geek a good reputation and name recognition. You might think of it as very effective free advertising. And at the websites of many free programs, the same company may offer paid versions with more capabilities and features. But don't think that means that the freeware version is not any good. Far from it.

Here are some of Rick's recommendations (for the IBM standard). He has used these programs for more than five years and has had no problems with any of them.

Treepad Lite

This is perhaps the best note taker, outliner, and notes organizer ever devised. As a text-based program, notes can be cut and pasted in virtually any other program (including Microsoft Word), emails, and Web pages.

www.treepad.com/treepadfreeware

IrfanView

IrfanView is one of the very best picture viewers, editors, organizers, and slide show creators around (plus it has dozens of more capabilities). At the IrfanView website, the company claims it is "one of the most popular viewers worldwide!"

www.irfanview.com

PROMOTIONAL ITEMS

- *You may be surprised at the number and quality of free promotional products that are available.*

Stores and services love to give away products with their name on it. We have seen pads of paper, ballpoint pens, small flashlights, sturdy cloth tote bags, key chains, coffee mugs, coolers, clocks, calculators, tape measures, screwdrivers, road atlases, multitools, tool kits, pocketknives, ice scrapers, emergency kits, magnifiers, and tire pressure gauges—just to name a few of the things you can find for free.

When you are at a hardware or auto store, for example, ask the clerk what freebies they have at the moment. You might be pleasantly surprised at what you can find.

CONSUMER BOOKLETS

Some of the very best and most reliable information comes from the U.S. government in easy-to-read and -understand booklets (yes, that's right!). Before the Internet, these were available only on paper from the Federal Citizen Information Center of the U.S. General Services Administration, in Pueblo, Colorado (if you're old enough you'll remember all the TV ads for this resource), and there was a nominal charge for many of these. Now, however, these are free online documents that you can print out at home. You can also order them on paper for the same pre–Information Age nominal fee. The wealth of really good consumer information at this site is staggering. Go to www.pueblo.gsa.gov.

You can find a treasure trove of booklets that will save you money on just about everything including cars, computers, food, health, housing, and travel. The complete Consumer Information Catalogue is available free in print form or online in PDF format. The catalog is updated quarterly and lists about two hundred publications.

HOW TO COMPLAIN—FREE COMPREHENSIVE BOOK FROM THE HORSE'S MOUTH

Imagine if you could get a 176-page book from the most authoritative source for free. This complete book would tell you everything you needed to know about how to get a complaint resolved including sample letters and checklists. Well, wait no longer. The 2008 *Consumer Action Handbook* is published by the U.S. government and is a gold mine for how-to complaint information. Go to the consumer action government site: http://www.consumeraction.gov. Then click on the link to order your free book. You can order one or two copies at a time. A PDF file is also available at the same website. This free publication should be on the bookshelf of every family and referred to when trying to resolve a complaint.

AUTOMOBILE REPAIR TOOLS

Some auto parts stores will loan you tools for free. You may be required to leave a deposit when you take the tool. For example, AutoZone (www.autozone.com) has a free "Loan-A-Tool Program" that includes a "complete selection of seldom-used, expensive-to-own specialty tools." The company website goes on to say, "60 different tools for all sorts of jobs—steering and suspension work, air-conditioning jobs, engine repair, and more. Using our Loan-A-Tool service is easy. Just leave a deposit at the store when you pick up the tool. When you're through, just bring it back, and we'll refund the deposit." A complete listing of the available tools by category is posted on the company's website. Or you can stop by your local store and ask an AutoZoner for assistance.

iPOD REPAIR

- *Free advice for iPod repair is available online.*

If you haven't got a warranty on your dysfunctional iPod, log on to www.fixya.com for free how-to-fix-it advice. The site posts free advice for iPods as well as other electronic items. If you don't see your problem there, just post a question and an answer will come your way.

Summary: Money-Saving Tips for Freebies

- Look for free calendars and record-keeping books.
- Get free software (freeware).
- Always look for free promotional items in stores.
- Get free consumer booklets from the U.S. government.
- Check out free auto repair tools.
- Find free iPod repair tips online.

A DOLLAR SAVED IS A DOLLAR EARNED (MAYBE MORE!)

At a barbecue the other day, a friend of Rick's asked about his money-saving tips. This same person had dismissed Rick's ideas for cheaper living a couple of years earlier, saying that they were not important. But now he was very interested. "I've got to save every penny," he said, "now that I'm not earning as much." Rick added, "There are two sides to the money coin—earning and saving. So in the end saving is like getting a really good, well-paying job that you can do when you like."

Way back when, Ben Franklin wrote, "A penny saved is a penny earned." With inflation that penny might really be a dollar's worth. But in any case the point is clear. When you save a dollar, it is the same as earning a dollar.

But saving that dollar may actually be more than a dollar earned, and here's why. When you save a dollar you do not have to pay income taxes or FICA. When you save a dollar on a product you buy, you save sales tax. When you save a dollar and don't put that dollar on a credit card, you save the interest on that borrowed dollar—well, you get the idea. So maybe a dollar saved is one dollar and fifty cents earned.

We believe that saving money is like getting a substantial pay raise. Plus, you don't have a boss leaning over your shoulder as you work. It's work you do for yourself and your family.

And you can put those savings together (as we have outlined in this book) to suit your own lifestyle and free time. What could be easier?

Saving money also gives you more control and puts you in charge of your own finances. You can decide not to spend an unnecessary $1,800 on food at the supermarket and instead use that money for other things. You can go on time-of-use at your local utility and save $600 a year—and then have the wonderful task of deciding how to spend it.

Saving money should not be a chore, once you've got the hang of it. And, as we have pointed out, it should not take any more time or extra work once you know how.

Saving money, in fact, is your royal road to financial freedom.

EXAMPLES OF POSSIBLE $5,000 HOUSEHOLD SAVINGS

Here's how one typical family might save $5,000 with our tips. Every household budget will be different: Some will save more in a category and others less, and many will save in categories not mentioned.

Example of Savings for a Typical Household

Store-brand food	=	$1,200
Store-brand clothing on sale	=	$200
Discount bin clothing at brand-name store	=	$200
Utility savings (for example, TOU)	=	$600
Filling up oil tank in August	=	$100
Hotel savings	=	$200
Foreign phone calls	=	$200
Raising insurance deductible	=	$400
Getting lower-priced insurance	=	$400
Credit card interest reduction	=	$500
Haggling for a big-ticket item (for example, refrigerator)	=	$200
Planning for purchase during seasonal sale	=	$200
Complaint resolution	=	$100
Restaurants	=	$200
Gasoline	=	$200
Prescriptions and OTC drugs	=	$300
Total savings for this family	=	$5,200

Example of Savings for a Retired Couple

Store-brand food	=	$1,000
Closeout food	=	$200
Store-brand clothing on sale	=	$200
Filling heating oil tank in August	=	$100
Hotel/travel savings	=	$700
Switching to prepaid cell	=	$400
Raising insurance deductibles on car/house	=	$400
Credit card interest reduction	=	$500
Planning for seasonal sales	=	$500
Complaint resolution	=	$300
Restaurants	=	$400
Gasoline	=	$100
Prescriptions/medicine	=	$900
Total savings for this family	=	$5,700

ACKNOWLEDGMENTS

My thanks to the editorial team at Random House, particularly Courtney Turco.

—Tom Philbin

NOTES

INTRODUCTION

xiii   your family's income has stayed flat: Tami Luhby, "Middle class: 'On the edge,'" CNN, July 24, 2008, http://money .cnn.com/2008/07/23/news/economy/middle_class/?post version=2008072407: "Adjusted for inflation, median household income dropped by $1,175 between 2000 and 2007, said Elizabeth Warren, professor at Harvard Law School, in written testimony before the Joint Economic Committee [of the United States House and Senate]."

xiii   while at the same time prices have been skyrocketing: Ibid.: "the average family is spending $4,655 more on basic expenses, such as gas, housing, food and health insurance. Gas alone costs $2,195 more for a family making the same commute in May 2008 as it did eight years earlier."

xiii   Americans already work one hundred hours longer per year: Porter Anderson, "Study: U.S. employees put in most hours," CNN, August 30, 2001, http://archives.cnn.com/ 2001/CAREER/trends/08/30/ilo.study/: "Workers in the United States are putting in more hours than anyone else in the industrialized world," said Lawrence Jeff Johnson of the United Nations' International Labor Organization (ILO). In 2001 Americans worked 1,978 hours on average. Australian, Canadian, Japanese worked about 100 hours less a year than Americans while the Brits and the Germans got even more time off.

xiii "add to that the price of heating oil and propane gas":
"Energy Outlook: Can Things Get Any Hotter?" *Connecti-
cut Business News Journal,* July 7, 2008, http://www
.businessnewhaven.com/article_page.lasso?id=42127:
". . . [A] recent report by the federal Energy Information
Administration held out little hope for significant relief.
The agency predicted home heating oil customers in the
Northeast will pay an average $3.66 a gallon this year, up
93 cents a gallon, or 34 percent, from the 2007 average of
$2.73 a gallon."

PART 1: OVERALL SHOPPING TIPS

SHOPPING TIP #2: HAGGLE

6 Two years ago, 33 percent of Americans haggled: A.
Pawlowski, "No cash? No problem, if you barter," CNN,
September 2, 2008, http://www.cnn.com/2008/LIVING/
wayoflife/09/02/bartering.rise/index.html

6 that figure has gone up to 67 percent: Alana Semuels,
quoting Britt Beemer of America's Research Group, in
"More bargain shoppers coming to terms with haggling,"
Los Angeles Times, April 15, 2008, http://articles.latimes
.com/2008/apr/15/business/fi-haggle15

6 in a survey in late 2007: "Survey results: When bargaining
works best" and "How to bargain for almost anything,"
ConsumerReports.org, Consumers Union, November
2007, http://www.consumerreports.org/cro/money/
shopping/shopping-tips/how-to-bargain-11-07/overview/
how-to-bargain-ov.htm, and http://www.consumerreports
.org/cro/money/shopping/ shopping-tips/how-to-bargain
-11-07/survey-results/how-to-bargain-survey-results.htm

6 You can haggle virtually anywhere: Bill Ritter, "Haggling
101: Finding Hidden Deals," ABC *20/20,* April 11, 2008,
http://abcnews.go.com/Business/story?id=4610552&page=
1. Coauthor Rick Doble was interviewed by ABC's *20/20*
and documented a recent haggled discount at Kmart. In
the same interview Teri Gault discussed haggling a discount at Macy's and Best Buy.

6   The experience of Jay Lyons: Interview with Jay Lyons by coauthor Tom Philbin. This was when Philbin became aware that haggling can be done with big companies.

7   In general, big-ticket items carry: See Tom Philbin's *Do-It-Yourself Bargain Book* (New York: Warner Books, 1992).

8   ask for a "painter's discount": Tom Philbin worked in the paint department at one point in his life and knows this tip as an insider.

8   about 50 percent of all patients: "Haggling with Health Care Providers About Their Prices Likely to Increase Sharply as Out-of-Pocket Costs Rise," Harris Interactive, *Healthcare News,* March 6, 2002, http://www.harrisinteractive.com/news/newsletters/healthnews/HI_HealthCareNews2002Vol2_Iss05.pdf

9   "The typical insurer gets": Emily Brandon, "5 Ways to Lower Your Medical Bills," quoting Gerard Anderson, director of the Johns Hopkins Center for Hospital Finance and Management, *US News & World Report,* November 29, 2007, http://www.usnews.com/articles/business/your-money/2007/11/29/5-ways-to-lower-your-medical-bills.html

9   You can also get food: Rick Doble, original research by his publication, *Savvy-Discounts Newsletter,* www.savvy-discounts.com

9   For a discount on new clothing and shoes: Andy Dappen, *Cheap Tricks* (Brier, Wash.: Brier Books, 1992), p. 102.

10 While you naturally will be thinking cash: Interview by Tom Philbin with Pete Prianti, who got a free $600 headboard.

SHOPPING TIP #3: TAKE ADVANTAGE OF LOW-COST STORE BRANDS

14 Wal-Mart has almost thirty: Wikipedia, "List of Wal-Mart Brands," October 19, 2008, http://en.wikipedia.org/wiki/Wal*Mart_Brands

SHOPPING TIP #4: BEST DEALS ARE IN A STORE'S SPECIALTY

16 Rick compared the price: Research by Rick Doble and his staff, *Savvy-Discounts Newsletter,* http://www.savvy-discounts.com/price_compare/comparison_pricing_6_0.htm

16   compared the cost of nonfood items: http://www.savvy
-discounts.com/price_compare/comparison_pricing_7_1
.htm

16   When he compared pharmacy prices: http://www.savvy
-discounts.com/price_compare/comparison_pricing
_8_0.htm

SHOPPING TIP #5: DON'T BUY EXTENDED WARRANTIES

17   "Most extended warranties": Fox Business Network,
"Extended Warranty Rip-Offs," September 06, 2005,
http://www.foxbusiness.com/story/personal-finance/
lifestyle-money/consumer-debt/extended-warranty-rip-offs

SHOPPING TIP #6: COMPLAIN WHEN NECESSARY

20   Look on the Internet: Most attorney general offices have a
consumer complaint division. While it is beyond the scope
of this book to list each state attorney general's Web address, you can easily find that office in your home state
along with the department (or division or bureau or other
name) that handles consumer complaints by searching for
"[state] attorney general consumer complaint." Many of
these websites will have a form that allows you to file a
complaint online.

SHOPPING TIP #7: TAKE ADVANTAGE OF SEASONAL SALES

22   Here is a roundup of seasonal sales: Rick Doble, original
research by *Savvy-Discounts Newsletter,* www.savvy-
discounts.com

SHOPPING TIP #9: BEWARE THE "MONEY-BACK GUARANTEE" SCAM

29   "PowerPurify" product offers: http://www.powerpurify.com/
?page=customer: "If you are dissatisfied with your purchase, you may cancel your new order for any reason for a
full product refund within 30 days of purchase (shipping
and handling charges are not refunded)."

SHOPPING TIP #11: DON'T BUY WHAT YOU DON'T NEED

32   every American is exposed: Advertising Industry Research
      Essentials, American Association of Advertising Agencies,
      "How Many Advertisements Is a Person Exposed to in a
      Day?," March 2007, http://www.aaaa.org/eweb/upload/
      FAQs/adexposures.pdf

SHOPPING TIP #14: BEWARE STORE TRAPS AND IMPULSE BUYING

36   wanted to find out if drugstores: Rob Eder, "Pharmacy
      Checkstand Is Prime Spot to Encourage Impulse Pur-
      chases," *Drug Store News,* November 4, 2002, http://
      findarticles.com/p/articles/mi_m3374/is_15_24/ai_94131817

SHOPPING TIP #15: BEWARE PRODUCT PLACEMENT IN MOVIES AND ON TV

38   Brands worldwide spent $3.07 billion: Lacey Rose, "James
      Bond: Licensed to Sell," *Forbes,* November 16, 2006,
      http://www.forbes.com/2006/11/16/bond-movie-
      advertising-tech-media-cx_lr_1116bond.html

38   James Bond movie *Die Another Day:* Jane Weaver, "License
      to Shill," MSNBC, November 17, 2002, http://www.msnbc
      .msn.com/id/3073513

38   In Steven Spielberg's movie *E.T.*: "A Product-Placement
      Hall of Fame," BusinessWeek.com, June 11, 1998,
      http://www.businessweek.com/1998/25/b3583062.htm

SHOPPING TIP #16: MISCELLANEOUS SHOPPING AND BUYING STRATEGIES

40   Hidden costs, such as bank fees: Bob Sullivan, *Gotcha Cap-
      italism* (New York: Ballantine, 2007). Sullivan examines
      how hidden fees are rampant in today's marketing.

41   an ad by Southwest Airlines: *USA Today,* September 26,
      2008. *USA Today* on August 12, 2008, included a compari-
      son chart, "From Booking to Onboard Snacking, Rising
      Airline Fees Add Up," which detailed the add-on charges of
      fifteen airlines and showed that most had fees for nineteen

different categories while Southwest charged only in three categories, such as for a third checked bag.

PART 2: INSIDERS' TIPS FOR SAVING MONEY ON SPECIFIC PRODUCTS AND SERVICES

CHAPTER 1: AUTOMOBILE EXPENSES

47 The Environmental Protection Agency (EPA) has tested: "Facts for Consumers 'Gas-Saving' Products: Fact or Fuelishness?," Federal Trade Commission, September 2006, www.ftc.gov/bcp/edu/pubs/consumer/autos/aut10.shtm

47 "zone pricing": Elizabeth Douglass and Gary Cohn, "Zones of Contention in Gasoline Pricing," *Los Angeles Times,* June 19, 2005, http://www.latimes.com/news/local/valley/la-fi-calprice19jun19,1,5304103.story?page=1&coll=la-editions-valley

48 on the same day in mid-June 2008: Comparison of one day's range of gas prices by Rick Doble using www.gasbuddy.com, a website that links to data about observed gas station prices.

49 How much gas can cruise control save?: "Fuel Economy, We Test the Tips, What Really Saves Gas? And How Much?," Philip Reed and Mike Hudson, Edmunds.com, November 22, 2005, http://www.edmunds.com/advice/fueleconomy/articles/106842/article.html

49 "Shell V-Power was carefully designed": "All About Shell V-Power®," http://www.shell.com/home/content/usa/products_services/on_the_road/fuels/shell_vpower/about_vpower/about_tabs.html

49 "using a higher-octane gasoline": "Facts for Consumers: The Low-Down on High Octane Gasoline," Federal Trade Commission, October 2003, http://www.ftc.gov/bcp/edu/pubs/consumer/autos/aut12.shtm

50 "most experts say excess octane": Tom and Ray Magliozzi, "Driving Tips For Tree Huggers," *Car Talk,* NPR, www.cartalk.com/content/eco/tips.html

51 the average driver can boost: Ibid.

53 nearly 17 percent of cars: Lisa Wade McCormick, "Rising Gas Prices Drive Search for Savings: Scams Abound, but So

Do Some Simple Gas-Saving Measures," ConsumerAffairs
.com, May 5, 2008, http://www.consumeraffairs.com/
news04/2008/05/gas_prices228.html

54 "parts changers": reader response to an article about auto
repair fraud in *The Virginian-Pilot,* July 1, 2008, http://
hamptonroads.com/2008/07/owner-three-auto-repair
-shops-gets-10-years-fraud: " 'parts changers,' which are
mechanics that change parts until they come to the defec-
tive part, and leave on the vehicle what they really didn't
need to change, and still charge the customer, THIS is too
common in the trade." Comment submitted by
joem69076 on July 1, 2008.

55 tires that are six years old: Joseph Rhee and Asa Eslocker,
"Aged Tires Sold as 'New' by Big Retailers," *ABC News,*
May 9, 2008, http://abcnews.go.com/Blotter/story?id
=4822250&page=1

56 "Old tires also are subject to greater stress": "Consumer
Advisory: Motorists Urged to Check Tires Before Summer
Trips," Press release, National Highway Traffic Safety Ad-
ministration, June 2008, http://www.safetyresearch.net/
Library/NHTSA_Advisory_Aging.pdf

56 "The age of the tire can be determined": Ibid.; see also
Erdem Uygar, "Tire Manufacture Date: How to Find It?,"
http://www.tuninglinx.com/html/car-tire-date-code.html:
"The first 2 digits is 'PRODUCTION WEEK' and the last 2
digits is the 'YEAR.' Assuming there are 4 weeks in a
month, we can say that this tire [with the date number
1203] was manufactured by the end of March 2003 (12=12th
week of the year, 03=Year 2003)."

57 "there is no question that buying a used car is always
cheaper": Tom and Ray Magliozzi, "Dear Tom and Ray,"
Car Talk, NPR, October 1997, www.cartalk.com/content/
columns/Archive/1997/October/05.html

58 "look through the very detailed repair reports": Toward
the back of every annual *Consumer Reports Buying Guide* is
an auto reliability section that lists about two hundred
makes and models going back about eight years. Reliability statistics are listed for sixteen different categories of
automobile trouble spots such as the engine, brakes, and

transmission. Your library may have a number of these annual reports.

62 "Edmunds True Cost to Own": "True Cost to Own (TCO)," http://www.edmunds.com/ apps/cto/CTOintroController. Edmunds says, "The Edmunds Inc. True Cost to Own (TCO) pricing system calculates the additional costs you may not have included when considering your next vehicle purchase. These extra costs include: depreciation, interest on your loan, taxes and fees, insurance premiums, fuel costs, maintenance, and repairs."

62 a tactic called "Opportunity Pricing": Brian Grow and Keith Epstein, "The Poverty Business: Inside U.S. companies' Audacious Drive to Extract More Profits from the Nation's Working Poor," *BusinessWeek*, May 21, 2007, http://www .businessweek.com/magazine/content/07_21/b4035001.htm

64 "When you have paid off the lease, you own nothing": Interview in 1997 by Rick Doble with Leslie Byrne, director of the U.S. Office of Consumer Affairs, about car leases for Doble's publication *Savvy-Discounts Newsletter*, www.savvy-discounts.com

65 your state's insurance department: Like the attorneys general offices for each state, it is beyond the scope of this book to list every state's insurance department. We suggest you search the Internet for "[your state] department of insurance" but also be aware that in some states this section of government might be an office or a division (not a department). Yet, as far as we know, there is one such office in each state. When you do locate the office in your state, look for the consumer section, since this office does a number of things, such as regulating and licensing insurance companies. Lastly, when you have found the consumer section, look for an "auto insurance comparison" area, where you will usually find a detailed and unbiased listing of the cost of different companies for typical driver profiles in a number of different areas of the state.

66 "the most effective antitheft device": Tom and Ray Magliozzi, "Dear Tom and Ray," *Car Talk*, NPR, September 1995, http://www.cartalk.com/content/columns/Archive/ 1995/September/13.html

CHAPTER 2: BANKING

69   "The FDIC insures $100,000": Nancy Trejos, "How the Banking Crisis Affects Consumers," *Washington Post,* July 16, 2008. Quote of a statement by Eric Solis, a certified financial planner, in an interview, http://www .washingtonpost.com/wp-dyn/content/discussion/2008/ 07/15/DI2008071502262_pf.html

71   "Checks were a high-profit item": John H. Harland Company history, in *International Directory of Company Histories,* vol. 17 (Farmington Hills, Mich.: St. James Press, 1997), http://www.fundinguniverse.com/company-histories/John-H-Harland-Company-Company-History.html

72   Don't order third-party checks at the last minute: Catherine Philbin (Tom Philbin's wife) provided this tip, and it's well worth heeding. Ordered checks can take two to three weeks to arrive. If necessary, you can get some checks at the bank to tide you over.

72   "Washington Mutual has such a card without a fee": The rules by which various banks charge fees vary. The best bet is to sit down and have a conversation with one of the bank's officers to find out precisely what the policy is.

73   If you can pay your bills later without a penalty: This is a good idea, but talk to the bank to make sure you know the drop-dead due date for your payment. It can get tricky. For example, you may pay online on a due date, but the bank won't credit it until the next day or two—and you'll be late.

75   "the average refund was $2,324": "Mind over Money: 10 Ways to Stash Cash," *Reader's Digest,* June 2008, http://www.rd.com/advice-and-know-how/saving-money-during-hard-financial-times/article58346-3.html

CHAPTER 3: CABLE TELEVISION

76   cable rates went up 93 percent: "Why is my cable TV bill going up so fast?," John W. Schoen, MSNBC, 2007.

76   typical prices increased 7 percent: Mark Cooper, "Cable Mergers, Monopoly Power and Price Increases," Consumer

Federation of America and Consumers Union, January 2003, http://www.consumersunion.org/pdf/ CFA103.pdf

CHAPTER 4: CLOTHING

82   But the real kicker is the price: Andy Dappen, *Cheap Tricks* (Brier, Wash.: Brier Books, 1992), p. 102.

82   "Sharon Stone Stunned Hollywood": "Divine Inspirations," *People,* September 15, 1997, http://www.people.com/ people/archive/article/0,,20123194,00.html

83   once new clothes have been washed: Amy Dacyczyn, *The Tightwad Gazette* (New York: Villard Books, 1993), p. 188.

83   clothing is available in irregulars: Tom Philbin, *Get More for Your Money* (New York: Fawcett Gold Metal, 1975). This was the first money book penned by Tom Philbin, and the message here is to be careful about buying "irregulars."

85   possible to buy clothing direct: Ibid.

CHAPTER 5: CREDIT AND CREDIT CARDS

87   slash your interest rate with a single call: "Want a lower credit card rate? Just ask," Lucy Lazarony, Bankrate.com, 2003.

88   Balance Liquidation Program: This program is not well-known; Rick stumbled across it when he was negotiating a lower interest rate with JPMorgan Chase and was presented with an offer by Chase to join this program. However, readers of this book might be able to call up Chase and initiate a discussion about this program now that they know what to ask for.

89   many people testified: Testimony of Consumer Action, Linda Sherry, editorial director, "Industry Practices of Credit Card Issuers," before the Senate Committee on Banking, Housing and Urban Affairs, May 17, 2005, http://banking.senate.gov/public/_files/sherry.pdf

95   average household has about $99: "99 dollars the amount of loose change each American has, says Coinstar," http://findarticles.com/p/articles/mi_m0846/is_/ai_n2545 0637

CHAPTER 6: DRUGS AND PRESCRIPTIONS

96   "The United States has the highest drug prices": "The Prescription Drug Fairness for Seniors Act: Industry Myths vs. Reality," prepared by Minority Staff, Committee on Government Reform, U.S. House of Representatives, April 10, 2001.

96   many seniors have to choose between: Health Care Costs Survey, USA Today/Kaiser Family Foundation/Harvard School of Public Health, survey conducted April 25–June 9, 2005.

96   many Americans have resorted: Jake Ulick, "Canada Drug Crackdown: Buying Cheap Drugs North of the Border May Become More Difficult," CNNMoney.com, March 13, 2003.

97   "Generic drugs are identical to their brand-name counterparts": Generic Initiative for Value and Efficiency, U.S. Food and Drug Administration, www.fda.gov

97   "the average price of a generic prescription drug": "Saving Money on Prescription Drugs," U.S. Food and Drug Administration, www.fda.gov

97   "generic drugs cost about 30 percent to 80 percent less": FDA Key Initiatives, U.S. Food and Drug Administration, www.fda.gov

97   In other words more than 75 percent of the drugs: "Saving Money on Prescription Drugs," U.S. Food and Drug Administration, www.fda.gov

99   "a very similar member of the same drug class": Ibid.

100   After a drug has been on the market about 20 years: "Frequently Asked Questions on Patents and Exclusivity," U.S. Food and Drug Administration, www.fda.gov

101   Be aware of "DTC" or direct-to-consumer marketing: Jonathan H. Marks, "The Price of Seduction: Direct-to-Consumer Advertising of Prescription Drugs in the US," NC Medical Journal 64, no. 6 (November/December 2003), http://www.ncmedicaljournal.com/nov-dec-03/ar110311.pdf

101   doctors gave patients the drug they requested: "The Public on Prescription Drugs and Pharmaceutical Companies," USA Today/Kaiser Family Foundation/Harvard School of

Public Health, March 2008, http://www.kff.org/kaiserpolls/upload/7748.pdf

102   Before removing the drug in 2004: "Vioxx lawsuit," Reuters, April 20, 2007, http://www.reuters.com/article/health-SP/idUSN2036845020070423?pageNumber =1&virtualBrandChannel=0

105   UnitedHealthcare urged members: Leo W. Banks and Jim Nintzel, "Men Behaving Badly: Our Annual Recap of the Year Gone by Finds That 2006 Was the Year of Living Obnoxiously," *Tucson Weekly*, December 28, 2006, http://www.tucsonweekly.com/gbase/Currents/Content?oid=90738

105   gave pill-splitters to its policyholders: Ryan Nakashima, "Splitting Pills Chops Costs, Insurers Discovering," Associated Press, June 10, 2005.

107   Wal-Mart has been offering hundreds of generic: "$4 Prescriptions Program," Wal-Mart Stores, http://www.walmart.com/catalog/catalog.gsp?cat=546834. The website states, "The list of eligible drugs in the $4 Prescriptions Program—available at Wal-Mart, Neighborhood Market and Sam's Club pharmacies nationwide—represents up to 95 percent of the prescriptions written in the majority of therapeutic categories. The affordable prices for these prescriptions are available for commonly prescribed dosages for up to 30-day or 90-day supplies."

110   When we compared eleven OTC products at Kmart: Rick did a comparison of the cost of Kmart brand versus national brand OTC drugs and found a savings of 44 percent. See *Savvy-Discounts Newsletter,* http://www.savvy-discounts.com/price_compare/comparison_pricing_4_0.htm

CHAPTER 7: ENERGY BILLS

113   A good rule of thumb is to replace: This rule of thumb was extrapolated from data at the U.S. government website on Energy Efficiency and Renewable Energy. Older systems have typically a 68–72 percent AFUE (Annual Fuel Utilization Efficiency rating). New furnaces can have an AFUE of 95 percent. Switching from a 70 percent AFUE to 95 percent AFUE will result in savings of $26.32 per $100 previ-

ously spent, for example. See the data at "Your Home: Furnaces and Boilers," A Consumer's Guide to Energy Efficiency and Renewable Energy, U.S. Department of Energy, http://apps1.eere.energy.gov/consumer/your_home/space_heating_cooling/index.cfm/mytopic=12530

114 half of investor-owned utilities: Chris S. King, "The Economics of Real-Time and Time-of-Use Pricing for Residential Consumers," American Energy Institute, June 2001, http://www.americanenergyinstitutes.org/research/The%20Economics%20of%20Time-Based%20Pricing%20for%20Residential%20Consumers.pdf

116 can save an average of about $200 during the winter: "Cut Your Heating Costs!," *Good Housekeeping,* February 2008, p. 96.

117 do-it-yourself energy audits: The U.S. Department of Energy website offers its own do-it-yourself energy audit and advice on getting a professional energy audit. Go to http://apps1.eere.energy.gov/consumer/your_home/energy_audits

117 the electric company will pay you money: Rocky Mount, North Carolina, is just one example of a load management program that pays you money. For more details about their program, go to http://www.rockymountnc.gov/utilities/savings.html

126 "According to *Popular Mechanics:* Jim Gorman, "DIY Home: 19 Ways to Slash Your Utility Bill," *Popular Mechanics,* November 2008, p. 96.

CHAPTER 8: FOOD AND GROCERIES

131 compared prices of seventeen: Al Morch, "Off-the-Shelf Advice on Saving Money," *San Francisco Sunday Examiner and Chronicle,* August 5, 1984, http://wps.aw.com/aw_carltonper_modernio_4/21/5566/1424975.cw/content/index.html

131 Rick did his own research: See *Savvy-Discounts Newsletter,* http://www.savvy-discounts.com/price_compare/comparison_pricing_7_0.htm

131 on ABC's *Good Morning America:* The segment aired on May 17, 2008.

131   a family buys two or three products: This method was created by Rick and the staff of *Savvy-Discounts Newsletter*.

132   "slotting fees": The FTC defines slotting fees as follows:
"Slotting allowances are one-time payments a supplier
makes to a retailer as a condition for the initial placement
of the supplier's product on the retailer's store shelves."
See "FTC Releases Grocery Industry Slotting Allowance
Report," Federal Trade Commission, November 14, 2003,
http://www.ftc.gov/opa/2003/11/slottingallowance.shtm

135   It turned out the most expensive vodka: Ann Varney and
Bill Ritter, "Does Premium Vodka's Taste Live Up to Its
Price Tag?," ABC News, May 24, 2007, http://abcnews.go
.com/2020/story?id=3201973&page=1

136   supermarkets are physically designed: "See the Supermarket as Selling Machine," *Consumer Reports*, September
1993.

136   "every additional minute": Janice Lieberman, *Tricks of the
Trade* (New York: Dell, 1996), p. 113.

137   "30 percent of packaged goods have lost content": Bruce
Horovitz, "Shoppers Beware: Products Shrink but Prices
Stay the Same," *USA Today*, June 13, 2008, http://www
.usatoday.com/money/industries/food/2008-06-11
-shrinking-sizes_N.htm

139   "overall coupon redemption rates": Eric Reyes, "Redemption," *Revenue Magazine*, January/February 2007, p. 36,
http://www.revenuetoday.com/story/redemption-15

139   redemption rates were at 2 percent: *Promo*, 2001, http://
promomagazine.com/news/marketing_coupons_billion/

140   "a statewide survey revealed that shoppers": Press release,
San Bernardino County, California, November 25, 2003,
http://www.co.san-bernardino.ca.us/pressreleases/docs/
647scanningerrorsrelease11-25-03.doc.htm

143   some health food stores will also sell you: Rick interviewed
the former owner of a community health food store, who
gave him this tip.

143   Twenty-five percent of bottled water: "Is your bottled water
coming from a faucet?," Phil Lempert, *Today*, NBC, July 21,
2004, http://www.msnbc.msn.com/id/5467759/

145 These ads feature bowls brimming with cereal: "Food
     Marketing to Children and Youth: Threat or Opportunity?,"
     Institute of Medicine, National Academy of Sciences, De-
     cember 6, 2005, http://www.iom.edu/?id=31330&redirect=0
     and http://www.cspinet.org/new/200512062.html. "The
     study was requested by Congress and sponsored by the
     U.S. Centers for Disease Control and Prevention (CDC)."

145 These highly advertised products: "Guidelines for Respon-
     sible Food Marketing to Children," Center for Science in
     the Public Interest, January 2005, http://www.cspinet.org/
     marketingguidelines.pdf. This report states in its section
     "Additional Guidance for Retail Stores," "Do not position
     in-store displays for low-nutrition foods or place low-
     nutrition products on shelves at young children's eye
     level," which implies that this is a common practice.

145 young people in recent years: "Increased Snacking Poses
     Threat to US Children's Health," Medical News, Medscape,
     April 19, 2001.

145 "consumption of sweets and fizzy drinks rises": Camillo
     Francassini, "Proved: TV Leads to Junk Food Diet,"
     The Times (of London), April 9, 2006, http://www
     .commercialalert.org/news/archive/2006/04/proved
     -tv-leads-to-junk-food-diet

146 "nag factor": How Companies Target Children," Michelle
     Madison, Polaris, Inc., August 2, 2005, http://www.polaris
     -inc.com/articles/index.cfm?fuseaction=article&rowid=853

147 "Since 1985, we have sold": Quote from the American Bev-
     erage Corporation website, www.ambev.com

CHAPTER 9: GARDEN SUPPLIES

148 "Nurseries often run seasonal sales": Interview by Tom
     Philbin with Joseph Beck, landscaper.

148 large nurseries, which have tremendous overhead: Ibid.

149 When a tree is on sale: Interview by Tom Philbin with
     Howard Kim, landscaper.

149 You can get a good buy on peat moss: Interview with
     Joseph Beck.

150 Unlike many products, buying insecticide: Interview with Howard Kim.

151 suiting the seed: Interview with Joseph Beck.

CHAPTER 11: HEALTH CARE

158 U.S. health-care quality fell: "U.S. still flunks healthcare test, group says," Reuters, July 17, 2008, http://www.reuters.com/article/latestCrisis/idUSN17479749

160 The first tool is to haggle: " 'Haggling' with Health Care Providers About Their Prices Likely to Increase Sharply as Out-of-Pocket Costs Rise," Harris Interactive, Healthcare News, March 6, 2002, http://www.harrisinteractive.com/news/newsletters/healthnews/HI_HealthCareNews2002Vol2_Iss05.pdf

160 "you may get a 30 percent discount": Emily Brandon, "5 Ways to Lower Your Medical Bills," quoting Gerard Anderson, director of the Johns Hopkins Center for Hospital Finance and Management, *US News & World Report,* November 29, 2007, http://www.usnews.com/articles/business/your-money/2007/11/29/5-ways-to-lower-your-medical-bills.html

162 "balance billing": Chad Terhune, "Medical Bills You Shouldn't Pay," *BusinessWeek,* August 18, 2008, http://www.businessweek.com/magazine/content/08_36/b4098040915634.htm?chan=top+news_top+news+index_top+story

166 The AARP suggests you ask: "Working Out: Choose the Right Health and Fitness Club," AARP, http://www.aarp.org/health/fitness/work_out/a2003-03-06-healthclub.html

CHAPTER 12: HOLIDAY EXPENSES

170 "The average consumer expects": Kathy Chu, "A holiday spending budget can help avoid debt hangover," *USA Today,* November 24, 2005, http://www.usatoday.com/money/perfi/general/2005-11-24-mym-holidays-usat_x.htm

170 "jewelry stores make almost a third": Ibid.

171   that you learn to become aware: Kimberly Palmer, "How to Be a Self-Aware Shopper," *US News & World Report*, August 1, 2007, http://www.usnews.com/usnews/biztech/articles/070801/01companygames.tips.htm

171   to put consumers into a warm and fuzzy: Kimberly Palmer, "Overspending? Blame Your Nose," *US News & World Report*, August 1, 2007, http://www.usnews.com/usnews/biztech/articles/070801/01companygames.research.htm

172   "The average consumer doesn't understand": Palmer, "How to Be a Self-Aware Shopper."

173   At the CVS pharmacy: This deep-discount negotiation was witnessed by Tom Philbin.

CHAPTER 13: HOME IMPROVEMENT

178   telling you that you need a new roof: Interviews by Tom Philbin with two insiders: Ed Linstadt of Lindstadt Seamless Gutter and Bill Baessler, licensing director, Suffolk County, New York, Department of Consumer Affairs.

180   the larcenous chimney sweep: Interviews by Tom Philbin with Bill Baessler of the Suffolk County Department of Consumer Affairs; Mike Blake of the Durham, New Hampshire, Fire Department; Marilyn Heeke of the Chimney Safety Institute of America; and Kevin Rooney, Oil Heat Institute of Long Island.

182   keeping water out of the basement: Interviews by Tom Philbin with Rich Barako of UGL Industries, Ed Lindstadt of Lindstadt Seamless Gutters, and John Condon of the American Society of Home Inspectors.

184   arm yourself with a few facts about termites: Information in this section was provided by Mike Potter, professor of entomology at the University of Kentucky. For scads of additional information on termites, visit the excellent website http://www.ca.uky.edu/entomology

186   oversee, as much as possible, all aspects of building an asphalt driveway: Interview by Tom Philbin with Bill Baessler, Suffolk County Department of Consumer Affairs, and John Delaney.

187   When it comes to mold scams: Information in this section
      supplied by Pat Huelman, associate professor of the De-
      partment of Bio-feed Products at the University of Min-
      nesota, and Dr. David Callahan of the Centers for Disease
      Control and Prevention.

CHAPTER 14: INSURANCE

192   Government information provides reliable: See the note to
      chapter 1 regarding state insurance departments. On the
      consumer section of the website look for a "homeowner's
      insurance comparison" area where you will usually find a
      detailed and unbiased listing of the cost of different compa-
      nies for different types of homes in a number of different
      areas of the state.

194   "If you can afford to raise your deductible to $1,000":
      "Ways to Lower Your Homeowners Insurance Costs," In-
      surance Information Institute, Federal Citizen Information
      Center, U.S. General Services Administration, www.pueblo
      .gsa.gov

194   savings from this high deductible: After learning about
      this, Tom raised his deductible from $500 to $5,000 and as
      a result, $50 a month was slashed off his premium for an
      annual savings of $600.

194   As reported in USA Today: Sandra Block, "Two families
      find a little change can save a lot," USA Today, Septem-
      ber 26, 2008, http://www.usatoday.com/money/perfi/
      basics/2008-09-26-frugal-families-winners_N.htm. In the
      USA Today article, the Pivnicks shopped around for new
      policies for their cars and their home. They got the same
      policies with the same coverage and deductible from other
      companies at a much lower cost. They saved $235 a month.
      If they had raised their deductible they could have saved
      even more.

195   "file a complaint as soon as possible": Your state insurance
      department is the best place to go for filing a complaint
      against an insurance company. Generally there are online
      forms you can fill out for such a complaint; the department
      will keep track of the number of complaints against an in-

surance company. Also, if there are a lot of complaints, the department can fine the company or prevent it from doing business in the state. While some consumers might be hesitant, it really is in the company's best interest to settle a legitimate claim filed through the state insurance department as soon as possible.

195 "use it and lose it": Les Christie, "Homeowners Insurance: Use It and Lose It: Many Insurers Refuse to Renew Policies of Homeowners Who File Claims," CNN, June 3, 2005, http://money.cnn.com/2005/05/26/pf/insurance/use_it _lose_it/index.htm

196 Insurance adjusters often offer 30 to 60 percent less: "Report Details Fraudulent Claims-Adjustment Practices in Homeowner Insurance Industry," *Law and Insurance,* August 22, 2007, http://lawandinsurance.typepad.com/law _and_insurance/2007/08/index.html

197 the property-casualty insurance industry: David Dietz and Darrell Preston, "Home Insurers' Secret Tactics Cheat Fire Victims, Hike Profits," http://www.bloomberg.com/apps/ news?pid=20601170&refer=home&sid=aIOpZROwhvNI

CHAPTER 15: TELEPHONE

203 At the end of your contract you can haggle: Bob Tedeschi, "It's a Buyer's Market: Haggle," *Money,* July 25, 2008, http://money.cnn.com/magazines/moneymag/moneymag _archive/2008/08/01/105711590/index.htm

204 Every year contact your wireless provider: Sandra Block, "Two Families Find a Little Change Can Save a Lot," *USA Today,* September 26, 2008, http://www.usatoday.com/ money/perfi/basics/2008-09-26-frugal-families-winners_N .htm. In the *USA Today* article, the Pivnicks both switched and reorganized their cellphone plans to save about $140 a month for the family.

CHAPTER 16: TRAVEL

213 ask for a free upgrade: Rick has used this tactic many times for rental cars and hotels. More often than not he has been given an upgrade with little fuss.

214 How much is a frequent flier mile worth?: Michelle Higgins, "The Miles Pile Up; Their Value Declines," *New York Times,* July 13, 2008, http://www.nytimes.com/2008/07/13/travel/13pracfflierfees.html

CHAPTER 17: MISCELLANEOUS EXPENSES, A TO Z

Burglar Alarms

218 Police Chief Steve Fuchila says: Tessa Melvin, "Home Alarms Prompt a Response: Rules and Fines," *New York Times,* July 30, 1989, http://query.nytimes.com/gst/fullpage.html?res=950DE6D9113BF933A05754C0A96F948260

218 fees that range from $50: J. Morris, "Council Considers UDO Amendments, Fines for False Alarms," *Kannapolis Citizen,* April 16, 2008, http://kannapoliscitizen.com/general/2008/04/16/council-considers-udo-amendments-fines-for-false-alarms

218 Many police departments will provide: Call your local police department and ask them what services they have for home burglary prevention and what they recommend.

218 Or the homeowner can download: There are a number of checklists provided by local police departments and others. For example, the "Burglary Prevention Information" from the town of DeWitt, New York. http://townofdewitt.com/?pageID=311, or the "Preventing Home Burglaries" page from the police department of El Cerrito, California: http://www.el-cerrito.org/police/preventhomeburglaries.html

Cesspools

218 As with so many other products: Interview by Tom Philbin with Bill Baessler, Suffolk County, New York, Department of Consumer Affairs.

College Costs

221 federally subsidized Perkins loans: Federal Perkins Loan Program, U.S. Department of Education, http://www.ed.gov/programs/fpl/index.html. The website states, "The

Federal Perkins Loan Program provides low-interest loans to help needy students finance the costs of postsecondary education."

221 government PLUS loans: PLUS Loans (Parent Loans), Federal Student Aid, http://studentaid.ed.gov/PORTALS WebApp/students/english/parentloans.jsp. The website states, "Parents can borrow a PLUS Loan to help pay your education expenses if you are a dependent undergraduate student enrolled at least half time in an eligible program at an eligible school. PLUS Loans are available through the Federal Family Education Loan (FFEL) Program and the William D. Ford Federal Direct Loan (Direct Loan) Program."

Cosmetics

222 cosmetics may be marked up sixfold: Janice Lieberman, *Tricks of the Trade* (New York: Dell, 1996), p. 56.

Funerals

225 "a loved one": Christopher Solomon, "Plan a Funeral for $800 or Less," MSN Money, http://articles.moneycentral .msn.com/RetirementandWills/PlanYourEstate/HowTo PlanAFuneral.aspx

225 "This is like telling": Interviews by Tom Philbin with two individuals—one a writer for a funeral industry magazine, the other a funeral director—who prefer to remain anonymous because of the nature of the facts they provided.

Luggage

228 Luggage that travels the airlines: Interview by Tom Philbin with retailer Walter Leute.

Moving

230 Six Tips: Tom Philbin, *Moving Successfully* (Yonkers, N.Y.: Consumer Reports Books, 1994). The government no longer provides a watchdog over the moving industry, so following the advice given here is particularly important.

Printer Costs

232 Ever wonder why computer printers: Interview and information gathered by Tom Philbin. The information on Cartridge World was actually derived from a conversation with an employee at Staples, and was then checked out. Walgreens, the author knows, is one of a number of drugstores that will refill ink-jet cartridges. The authors believe that laser-jet cartridges are one of the big rip-offs of our time. Markup is probably much worse than jewelry. Advice: If you have a choice, buy an ink-jet printer. It's slow, but a lot cheaper than a laser printer.

RICK DOBLE is said to be the king of haggling. He has been teaching people how to haggle on his website (www.Savvy-Discounts.com/haggling) as well as in his *Savvy Discounts Newsletter* for the past ten years. He was one of the first consumer advocates to see how the demand for haggling savvy has grown, and he has been interviewed over one hundred times by print, radio, and TV media. Rick's advice has also been included in money-saving articles for magazines and newspapers such as *The Wall Street Journal, Reader's Digest, Woman's Day, Woman's World,* and *Bottom Line/Personal* and on television and radio outlets such as ABC's *20/20* and NPR.

TOM PHILBIN writes both fiction and nonfiction. Three of his earlier books were specifically aimed at helping consumers save money. They include *Your Money, Get More for Your Money,* and *Tom Philbin's Do-It-Yourself Bargain Book.* He is also the author of the *Library Journal* bestseller *How to Hire a Home Improvement Contractor Without Getting Chiseled.* He has made innumerable media appearances.